THE
COMING
HEALTH
CRISIS

THE
COMING
HEALTH
CRISIS

Who Will Pay for Care for the Aged in the Twenty-first Century?

John R. Wolfe

The University of Chicago Press

Chicago and London

John R. Wolfe is associate professor of economics at
Michigan State University

The University of Chicago Press, Chicago 60637
The University of Chicago Press, Ltd., London
© 1993 by The University of Chicago
All rights reserved. Published 1993
Printed in the United States of America

02 01 00 99 98 97 96 95 94 93   2 3 4 5 6

ISBN (cloth): 0–226–90515–2

Library of Congress Cataloging-in-Publication Data

Wolfe, John R.
The coming health crisis : who will pay for care for the aged in the
twenty-first century? / John R. Wolfe.
p.   cm.
Includes bibliographical references and index.
1. Medicare.   2. Aged—Medical care—United States—Finance.
3. Aged—Long term care—United States—Finance.   4. Age
distribution (Demography)   I. Title.
HD7102.U4W63   1993
368.3'82'00846—dc20   92-17098
                                                                        CIP

Figure 2.3 in Chapter 2 appeared as figure 2 in G. C. Meyers and K. G.
Manton, "Compression of Mortality: Myth or Reality," *The Gerontologist*
24, no. 4 (1984): 348. Copyright © The Gerontological Society of America.
Reprinted with permission.

CONTENTS

FIGURES AND TABLES

Figures

Tables

ACKNOWLEDGMENTS

The origin of this book was my own desire to broaden my knowledge of health and long-term-care insurance: in doing so, I spent more time combing public health libraries than I did reading economics journals. I am grateful to the Department of Economics and the College of Business at Michigan State University for granting me the luxury of a sabbatical year in which to enjoy undisturbed reading and writing, and to two anonymous reviewers for their very thoughtful suggestions. I am grateful also to Kari Foreback and Marneta Griffin for their patient and skillful assistance with the typing. Most of all I am grateful to my wife, Sandy Whitesell, whose faith and loving encouragement make the completion of this project and all my other ventures possible.

1

Introduction

IMAGINE THE United States in the year 2040. Almost a quarter of the population is aged 65 or older (versus only about one-eighth in 1990), and about 4% of Americans are aged 85 or older (versus only about 1% in 1990). Never has the demand for health and long-term care been so great: since 1990, the fraction of the population in nursing homes has roughly doubled, the fraction of the population with disabilities has risen by about two-thirds, and annual hospital stays per capita is about one-third higher. The Social Security Old Age, Survivors and Disability Insurance Trust Funds are about a year away from exhaustion, having been steadily depleted for the previous 25 years, and the Medicare fund used to pay hospital bills has long ago receded into history, having been exhausted in 2005.

As unsettling as this picture is, it is not merely possible: each of these predictions is in fact a best-guess forecast, based on assumptions of most likely economic and demographic trends[1] and of no change from current law. While uncertainty about the assumptions makes more favorable outcomes possible, it also makes an even greater aging of U.S. society and an even more rapid growth of demand for medical and long-term care equally likely. The Social Security and Medicare projections warn us that we, as a society, have not yet made adequate preparation to meet the staggering future needs that we in fact consider probable.

But how sensitive are these projections to what is assumed about long-term economic and demographic change? And, if we accept these or other projections as valid, how can policy intervention or changes in individual behavior alter the out-

1

come? Thoughtful planning requires that both questions be addressed. This volume attempts to do so.

At the heart of the problem is demographic change. Throughout most of the twentieth century, the birthrate in the United States has followed a gradual downward trend, and it is now slightly below the level needed to maintain a stable population size. The exception to this downward trend was the period beginning in the mid-1940s and ending in the late 1960s, during which the birthrate increased explosively and then returned to its previous path. The age distribution of the population remains starkly distorted in 1991: the number of 35-year-old Americans, for example, is currently about twice the number of 55-year-olds, but it also exceeds the number of 15-year-olds by about one-third.[2]

At each stage of its life, the so-called Baby Boom generation has had a disproportionate influence on American life and culture. In childhood it required massive investment in school construction and teacher training; in adolescence it introduced a powerful youth culture to the American scene and lent its weight to antiwar politics; and in young adulthood and middle age its preferences have dominated consumer markets and entertainment offerings.

But the Baby Boom generation's size has also brought it economic hardship. High school and college graduates in the 1970s and early 1980s found the labor market unable to readily absorb so many entry-level workers: relative shortages of supervisory senior-level workers and of capital made well-paying entry-level positions scarce. Even the lifetime value of a college degree fell when this largest, most-educated generation received their diplomas and began their search for jobs (Freeman 1986).

Economically, their preponderance relative to their elders does have a positive side: as their parents' generation ages, creating needs for intrafamily support and for transfers through government retirement programs, the great number of Baby Boomers among whom this burden is shared is making it easier for individuals to bear. But the same arithmetic has ominous implications for the future: as Baby Boomers age, the burden of transfers placed on their children and their children's children will, on a per worker basis, be several times greater than it is today.

Even in the 1970s and 1980s, with Baby Boomers still in midcareer, public transfer programs providing income support and medical insurance to the aged have experienced harrowing financial troubles. Old Age and Survivors Insurance (OASI), often called Social Security after the 1935 Social Security Act that created it, teetered on the edge of bankruptcy in 1983, and required tax increases and a six-month moratorium on cost-of-living adjustments to maintain promised benefit payments. OASI has been able to generate budgetary surpluses since 1983, in part by subjecting benefits to income taxes, but the surplus funds have in effect been borrowed by the U.S. Treasury to make up for cuts in other taxes. The interest that they earn is simply a tax liability for current and future workers, not a reflection of any embodiment in productive capital. And Health Insurance (HI), the portion of Medicare that provides the aged with insurance against hospital expenses, projects exhaustion of its trust fund in just 14 years, under best-guess assumptions (Board of Trustees, Federal HI Trust Fund, 1991), even though the oldest Baby Boomers will have attained only about 60 years of age by that date. And even under its optimistic set of assumptions, HI's Trust Fund would be exhausted by 2018. This makes prospects for succeeding decades bleak indeed.

This faltering system of transfers from young to old is the legacy of a past in which population was always expected to grow: when each generation begets a larger generation of offspring, it can expect to receive more in retirement transfers than it gave in its own working years. But Baby Boomers will outnumber their juniors; in fact, the total population of the United States has been projected by the Census Bureau to peak in the 2030s, at around 300 million, and then to begin a steady decline.[3]

Simultaneous with ups and downs in the birthrates there have been rapid increases in retirement life expectancy. Life expectancy at age 65 has increased by about two years since 1970, while the fraction of the population aged 85 or older has roughly doubled. Another two-year life-expectancy increase and another doubling of the fraction of the population aged 85 or older are possible by about 2030.[4] Rates of hospitalization and nursing home residency are highest by far at these most advanced ages, so that the costs of medical and long-term care for the aged have grown rapidly, straining the nation's productive capacity. These needs will keep expanding, as long as life expectancy continues to increase. By 2030, the Baby Boom population bulge will be gone from the work force, leaving thinning ranks of workers in its place, and will have begun to increase the populations of hospitals and nursing homes.

We cannot, of course, simply extrapolate mortality improvements into the future without recognizing a high degree of uncertainty. Changes in future decades depend in large part on developments in medical knowledge, technology, and care delivery as well as in lifestyle, nutrition, and fitness, all of which can barely be imagined today. Perhaps even more important, they will depend on interrelationships between aging, sickness, and death which are not yet well understood. Does the body wear out according to an internal clock which measures the years up to an immutable maximum life span, or can we increase the length of life without limit? When we reduce mortality from a single illness, do we typically also experience a drop in the incidence of that illness, or do we see instead a larger population of afflicted survivors? And to what extent are its survivors more susceptible than their peers to other illnesses? The size of the aged population, and rates of illness and disability in each age subgroup of that population, depend enormously on the answers to these questions; therefore, so, too, will demands for health and long-term care in the twenty-first century.

But projection of health and long-term-care needs is not simply a matter of forecasting the growth rates of age subgroups and weighting by their respective utilization rates. Allowance must also be made for improvement in the quantity and quality of care expected by successive generations of aged recipients. It is economic growth that makes such improvements possible. United States productivity has grown rapidly enough since the Great Depression to permit the average standard of living, as measured by real per capita disposable income, to roughly double every thirty years. But the coming decline in the proportion of the population that is working age could slow this growth. If so, which sectors of the economy will fall behind—those that provide care for the sick and the disabled, or those that meet the needs of others? This choice will confront hard-pressed younger workers as they consider tax increases to support growing transfer programs as soon as 20 years from now.

It is always especially prudent for those with the fewest children to save for retirement and possible infirmity, in order to minimize dependence on public largesse late in life. To date, Baby Boomers as a group show little sign of such prudent saving: in fact, the personal saving rate plunged in the 1980s and remains well below historical standards.[5] And government borrowing on an unprecedented scale further depresses national net savings.

Greater saving, by those who will retire after the first decade of the twenty-first century, would not only provide a nest egg but would also counter the effect of the decline of the work force, relative to population, with an increase in productive capital. The savings embodied in that capital would provide interest and dividends with which to augment scarce transfers from workers.

Retirement needs are predictable, and a prudent individual with sufficient preretirement income can save enough to meet those needs. It is, however, impossible for individuals to anticipate their uncertain future medical and long-term-care needs decades in advance. Furthermore, some will face catastrophic expenses for which they could not possibly save enough, while others will have so few medical and long-term-care expenses as to leave any saving earmarked for these purposes unused. For each to try to save enough to cover a worst case would be inefficient: fortunately, insurance can cover the same risks with fewer funds by pooling them. If this insurance coverage is prefunded, rather than paid for out of current income, then it contributes to capital formation and economic growth.

Medicare pools risks of hospitalization and could be used as a vehicle for savings accumulation: its payroll tax rate and its premium could be increased and the funds saved to be used decades from now. As a nearly universal social insurance program, Medicare enjoys scale economies and does not have to market policies or screen applicants, unlike decentralized private insurance. The current borrowing of Social Security surpluses to finance other federal spending gives reason to doubt, however, that the Medicare fund accumulation would translate into real capital accumulation. Moreover, while Medicare meets short-term acute care needs well, its coverage for other care is quite limited: for hospital stays of catastrophic length, Medicare places a cap on reimbursements, and it provides very little long-term care to those with chronic ailments or disabilities. For those without adequate private resources, the public assistance program called Medicaid takes over from Medicare to meet these catastrophic medical or long-term-care expenses. Medicaid has no trust fund, is conditioned on very low income and assets, and typically provides such low reimbursements as to place recipients at the back of the queue for care. In short, it is an unsuitable vehicle for fund accumulation.

Before Medicare, there was little health and long-term-care insurance for the aged; the markets that have developed have grown to fill in around it. The most well-developed is "medigap" insurance, which covers many of the acute medical care expenses left uncovered by Medicare. Unfortunately, medigap policies are not an ideal insurance product upon which to build expanded coverage. They usually cover Medicare's deductibles and coinsurance, encouraging overutilization, but are less likely to cover catastrophic expenses incurred by those who exceed Medicare's maximum-covered length-of-stay.

In the last five years, a private long-term-care insurance market also has emerged. The cost per person generally exceeds $1,000 annually, and, while sales have grown at a rapid rate, the policies sold to date still cover a very small fraction of those at risk for long-term-care expense. Others must spend what resources they have and then turn to Medicaid.

The growth of medical and long-term-care coverage for the aged is hindered by a number of problems, which are common to most insurance, but especially troublesome in these markets. Health risks vary widely among the aged population, and it is costly to assess the health of each applicant. Without a careful screen of customers, however, an insurer may end up insuring a population anticipating greater-than-average expenses, and be forced to price the coverage so high as to make it a bad buy for the average customer. In the case of long-term care, the dividing line between covered care and everyday living expense is indistinct, so that insurers must be careful to limit reimbursable expenses to those that are truly losses due to illness or injury, lest they allow insurance funds to displace part of the household's regular budget for food and shelter. Uncertain inflation in the future cost of care is one of the greatest risks of all, and this risk does not vary significantly among potential customers; the insurer can choose to bear it, at a price, but cannot lessen it by pooling. Wealth at the point of retirement is not easily liquidated to pay insurance premiums, since consumers at this stage of life typically have much of their wealth in real estate. Home ownership provides security, but also ties up more wealth than is really needed to pay for housing services for the remainder of one's life. And, finally, there are many in today's elderly population with scant resources even to meet more immediate expenses than insurance, especially among women living alone.

A number of innovative arrangements have been developed, in parallel with private long-term-care insurance, in order to alleviate these problems. The Social Health Maintenance Organization is a long-term-care insurance plan built upon the foundation of a prepaid medical plan. It takes advantage of the ability of an established health-care delivery system to build a balanced patient pool and to efficiently manage, provide, and limit care. The Continuing Care Retirement Community combines guaranteed lifetime residential, medical, and long-term-care services in a campus setting, financed by partial prepayment and premiums. This arrangement enables entrants to translate home equity into insurance equity and can offer them minimal disruption, should they need institutional care. Reverse Annuity Mortgages provide an alternative way for homeowners to use the equity in their homes to pay for insurance: unlike a move to a Continuing Care Retirement Community, a Reverse Annuity Mortgage provides funds while the owner remains at home, and the house becomes another's property only after a preagreed period of time has elapsed.

The goal of this volume is to summarize what we know about the changes to come in the age distribution of our population, the implications for a health-care and long-term-care delivery system which is now financed largely by intergenerational transfers, and the prospects for bolstering the role of prefunded insurance in that system. While it draws upon recent published work by specialists in the demography of aging, in geriatric public health, and in the economics of health and of risk and insurance, an effort has been made to keep the presentation accessible to interested professionals and lay people, regardless of their disciplines and backgrounds.

The organization of the remainder of this volume is as follows: Chapter 2 begins with a look at the generally adequate incomes of today's elderly, at the high concentration of poverty among the oldest singles, and at the importance of home ownership in the wealth of the elderly. Projections of the twenty-first-century age distribution are then considered in detail, and the roles of fertility, mortality, and morbidity trends are assessed. Competing theories relating progress against mortality to the health of survivors have especially profound implications for future utilization of care and are given special attention. Projected rates of growth of per capita medical and long-term-care demands are then compared to the likely range of future overall economic growth rates: long-term care is found to be the category of care most likely to outpace other production.

Chapter 3 begins by explaining how the adequacy of a system of transfers from workers to their retired elders depends primarily on rates of growth of population, of income, and of participation in that system. It then profiles, in turn, the current arrangements by which we finance medical and long-term care for the aged, highlighting the prominent role of public transfer programs in each. Coverages and financial structures of Medicare and Medicaid are described, their gaps in coverage highlighted, and their financial projections described and interpreted in the context of likely concurrent financial difficulties for the Social Security retirement program.

Chapter 4 describes problems that insurers must overcome if private medical and long-term-care insurance offerings are to expand. The first section describes adverse selection, the problem of the poorest risks having the greatest demand for insurance. After summarizing recent advances in economic modeling of the problem, adverse selection is then considered as a reason to mandate universal pooled insurance. Evidence of adverse selection in related markets is summarized, and inflation vulnerability is argued to be an intimately related problem. Moral hazard, the tendency of insurance to encourage the use of covered services, is given a parallel treatment, with conceptual arguments and empirical evidence presented in turn. The chapter concludes with a look at the problems posed by the prevalence of underfunded employer-based retirement health plans.

Chapter 5 reviews alternative proposals for meeting twenty-first-century medical and long-term-care needs. With regard to financing of medical care, possibilities range from maintaining Medicare's pay-as-you-go character to accumulating a larger trust fund. In either case, it will be necessary to find new revenue sources or to suppress the growth of spending; reduced reimbursement for low levels of care and the rationing of care on the basis of age are discussed as approaches to controlling spending. Possible approaches to long-term-care financing include introducing a block grant structure to Medicaid, mandating a new social insurance program, and promoting the growth of private insurance. The latter includes not only conventional policies but also prepaid care provided through Social/Health Maintenance Organizations and Continuing Care Retirement Communities. The potential roles of Individual Retirement Accounts and Reverse Annuity Mortgages as sources of funds for premiums and entrance fees are also addressed.

Finally, Chapter 6 summarizes what can be done to promote prefunded insurance and avert predicted future shortages of care.

2

Medical and Long-Term Care in the Twenty-first Century: Profile and Projection of the Aged Population

The Economic Status of the Aged

THE ELDERLY are now about as well-off financially as the non-elderly, on average, having had a much higher rate of income growth since the mid-1960s (Hurd 1990), and they remain at least as well-off after adjusting for age-related differences in in-kind assistance, taxes, net worth, and other factors not reflected in household income (Smeeding 1989). In fact, if we include in income the value to recipients of all noncash government benefits, of which Medicare is an especially large item for those over age 65, the overall poverty rate of the aged is actually lower than that for the remainder of the over-25 population. If we exclude Medicare, for the reason that high medical expenditures may not imply a high standard of living, the poverty rate of the over-65 population is the slightly higher one. Either way, the rate of poverty among the aged is lower than that of the overall population, because persons under age 25 are much more likely to be poor than their elders, taken together.[1] And at the same time that the aged have been making financial gains relative to others, they have enjoyed increasingly independent living and have been working less, due to earlier retirement (Palmer 1988).

But both aged and nonaged populations contain gender and marital status subgroups which differ strikingly in economic standing. Within the elderly population, poverty is highly concentrated among women without marital partners, and also among those farthest removed from the ages of peak earnings. In 1980, the poverty rate among the oldest old (85 and older) was almost twice as great as among the youngest old (65–69) (Rosenwaike 1985).

10

This relationship actually has more to do with marital status than with aging: the income distribution of persons living alone changes little with increasing age, but their predominance in older cohorts drives up poverty rates of those cohorts. In 1990, the poverty rate for women aged 65 or older living alone was 27%, and it was also high for aged men living alone (17%), although they are much less numerous. In contrast, the poverty rate for aged couples was only 6%.[2] Differential mortality may contribute to this economic stratification by marital status: husbands' mortality rates appear to be inversely related to income and wealth (Hurd 1990).

But aging and widowhood also give rise to age-related differences in earnings, in Social Security benefits, and in pension incomes (Atkins 1985). While a significant minority of workers continue to work in part-time transitional jobs through their late 60s, few do so in the later decades of life. Older retirees receive generally smaller Social Security benefits because benefits are scaled according to a worker's real earnings at the point of retirement: each birth cohort's benefits fall behind the secular growth in real wages of succeeding cohorts. Further, Social Security benefits for singles (which include widows and widowers) are only two-thirds of combined benefits for otherwise identical retired workers and their dependent spouses.

The increasing importance of private pensions has tended with the passage of time to widen the gap between the poor and the affluent elderly, since much of the older population remains uncovered (Palmer 1988). About half of the over-65 male population receives private pension benefits, but only about one-quarter of women over 65 do;[3] not only are women less likely to be covered in their own right, but some older widows also lose pension incomes upon the deaths of their spouses. Until the passage of the Retirement Equity Act in 1984, workers accruing pensions could decline joint-and-survivor coverage without the consent of their spouses, thereby obtaining higher pension benefits during their own lives. A study of retired couples in the late 1970s found that half of those eligible for joint-and-survivor coverage had declined it, and that poverty among eligible widows could have been halved had all eligible couples chosen joint-and-survivorships. Remarkably, poverty would not have increased among couples, despite the reduction in benefits for many intact couples (Myers, Burkhauser, and Holden 1987). Apparently, mandatory pension survivorship could reduce the number of wives who become poor upon the deaths of their husbands, and possibly without exacerbating poverty among any other subgroup.

As wealth holders, the greatest common denominator of the aged is home ownership. In 1980, 75% of the aged owned their homes, and only a small minority had outstanding mortgages on those homes. Yet only about half had other assets producing incomes of more than $500 per year (Atkins 1985). For those whose wealth is almost entirely tied up in housing, home equity conversions (discussed in Chap. 5) could annuitize unneeded future housing services into increased current income, but their potential is as yet largely untapped.

Mortality and Morbidity Trends

The Squaring of the Age Pyramid

It is widely recognized that the population of the United States is rapidly aging; few Americans would be surprised to hear that the age of the median member of the population has increased in recent years. It has risen, in fact, from about 28 in 1970 to about 33 in 1989.[4] Simple one-dimensional trends, however, disguise a multiplicity of demographic phenomena which are all part of a society's aging process. Both falling birthrates and death rates alter the age distribution of the population, but at opposite ends of the population's age spectrum. And also of great importance are changes in age-specific rates of sickness and disability: any improvements in the health and functional ability of the aged tend to mitigate the increasing dependency that otherwise results when mortality rates decline.

The aging of the population over the last 20 years has been the product of erratic fluctuations in both birthrates and death rates; changes in age-specific rates of disability and morbidity may also have occurred, but are not yet well understood. Figure 2.1 illustrates changes in the relative sizes of age cohorts, using intermediate-case projections produced by the Census Bureau (Spencer 1989). The figure depicts a gradual "squaring" of the "pyramid" indicating the sizes of successive age cohorts; the

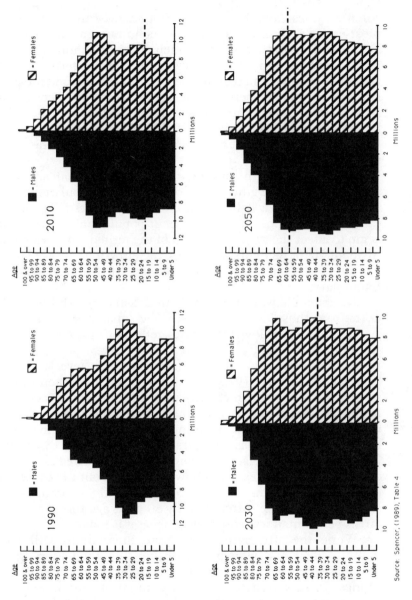

Figure 2.1 Projected age distribution of the U.S. population by sex and by selected years

Source: Spencer, (1989), Table 4

changing shape indicates younger cohorts outnumbering older cohorts by less and less. The role of changes in birthrates is most easily seen in comparisons of cohorts aged less than 60, before adult mortality has had much effect on cohort size. The pear-shaped pattern in 1990 reveals three major fertility fluctuations: a plunge in birthrates in the 1930s has made the pyramid roughly square between the ages of 50 and 70, then cohort sizes change rapidly between ages 30 and 50, due to the Baby Boom which peaked in the late 1950s. Finally, the subsequent Baby Bust has actually caused an inward tapering of the pyramid below age 30.

As the 1930s birth cohort enters old age, its small size will actually reduce the growth rate of the elderly population. The imbalance between Baby Boom and Bust cohorts is currently causing an aging of the preretirement population, but will not begin to affect the age distribution of the retired population until about 2010. As figure 2.1 shows, the growth of the aged population that is expected to ensue between 2010 and 2030 is extraordinary.

Horizontal dashed lines in figure 2.1 distinguish living cohorts from those unborn in 1990. The squareness of the projected pyramids below those lines reflects Census Bureau assumptions of roughly constant fertility rates, at a rate per woman remaining just below the replacement level as it has been since the early 1970s. Small increases since then in the sizes of successive birth cohorts were due entirely to increases in the number of potential mothers. Given the steadily downward long-term trend in the number of births per woman and its stability over the past 20 years, our best guess for the future is surely a below-replacement birthrate extrapolated ahead indefinitely. Nevertheless, we know too little about the causes of birthrate fluctuations to rule out the possibility of an upswing at some future time. After all, only 30 years ago the number of births per woman was about twice what it is today.

While the aftermath of birthrate fluctuations will profoundly affect our demographic future, the population aging that has occurred since 1970 is actually due primarily to changes in survival rates. Mortality improvements were especially rapid in the 1970s, after little improvement in the 1960s: for example, deaths per 100,000 75–84-year-old men only fell from 10,200 in 1960 to 10,000 in 1970, but plummeted to 8,800 by 1980.[5] This improvement in mortality has broadened the top of the age pyramid, and the rate of growth has been especially rapid among the "oldest old" population, a label now in common use to designate those aged 85 or older. Much of the improvement in the 1970s was due to reductions in mortality from two major killers, heart disease and stroke; the latter reduction was due in large part to improved treatment of hypertension. Reductions in mortality associated with pneumonia/influenza and hip fracture have also contributed to overall mortality improvements (Manton and Soldo 1985). Despite an increase in death rates due to cancer in the 1970s, life expectancy at 65 increased by more than a year during the same period, for both men and women.[6]

A recurrent theme in the literature on the growing population of the oldest old is their high degree of heterogeneity. In their review of published evidence, Riley and Bond (1983) found a great variability in physiological rates of aging, and Minaker and Rowe (1985) argue as clinicians that the variability of disease is greater the older the population. One implication is that older persons who are ill have a greater need for costly individualized care and attention than younger patients.

Another implication of heterogeneity is that aging may actually change the character of an age cohort, because to subject a heterogeneous population to survival hazards leads to a highly selected cohort of survivors. As an example, cancer and diabetes death rates decline with age at the oldest ages; this suggests selection at younger ages of the most susceptible to those ailments. Similarly, the rate of disability among the noninstitutionalized population declines between ages 85 and 90; this suggests that nursing home admission and death at younger ages select out those most prone to disablement.

As the relative size of the elderly population increases, so does the prevalence in the population of conditions associated with old age. In addition to killer diseases such as cancer, and chronic nonfatal ailments such as cataracts, these include geriatric syndromes like memory loss and urinary incontinence. By making family or institutional care necessary, the latter conditions can be as costly of resources as fatal illnesses. Urinary incontinence, for example, has been estimated to account for as much as 20% of the total cost of nursing home care (Minaker and Rowe 1985). The personal care needs of those aged 85 and older are especially great: 40% need assistance walking, and another 30% need help with some other normal daily activity, compared to only 5% and 10%, respectively, for the population aged 65–74 (Rosenwaike 1985). The proportion of the elderly population that is institutionalized also increases very rapidly with age: in 1980, only 2% of those aged 65–74 were institutionalized, compared to 23% of those aged 85 or older. The latter figure had also more than doubled in thirty years with most of that increase taking place before 1970 (Rosenwaike 1985).

Because of women's lower and more rapidly improving mortality rates at older ages, the elderly population is predominantly female and has been increasingly so. This is most evident in the population aged 85 and older, where the ratio of men to women has declined from 0.75 in 1940 to 0.44 in 1980. As a result, widowhood is by far the most common situation of women who have survived beyond age 85; in 1980, only 33% of women aged 65–69, but 82% of those 85 and older, were widowed. In contrast, almost half of men over 85 remained married, while only 44% were widowed (Rosenwaike 1985.)

Above the dashed lines in figure 2.1, the breadth of the age pyramid depends not only on past fertility but also on assumptions about survival rates decades from today. Because the effects of mortality improvements accumulate with age, the projected sizes of cohorts are increasingly sensitive to mortality assumptions the older the cohort. And the Census Bureau projections in figure 2.1 do show very rapid secular increases in the sizes of the oldest age cohorts. While the total population is projected to increase by about one-fifth between 1990 and 2030, the population over age 65 is projected to increase by a factor of about two, and the population over age 85 by a factor of about two-and-a-half. Yet underlying this forecast of enormous growth among the oldest old is the assumption of a return to less rapid mortality improvement than was experienced in the 1970s and early 1980s (Spencer 1989).

Because the oldest old are the most intensive users of medical and long-term care, their numbers are a most critical element of any forecast of future costs. Yet their projected population is extremely sensitive to mortality assumptions. Guralnik, Yanagishita, and Schneider (1988), for example, projected that a continuation of mortality declines comparable to those in the 1970s would increase the population over age 85 in 2040 to almost double the number projected by the Census Bureau.

Such projections have been the subject of heated debate in the 1980s, however, as the mortality fluctuations of the last few decades have stimulated scholars to formulate competing models of the process of aging and death. Much of the debate was touched off by Fries (1980, 1983), who argued that the age of 85 is an approximate upper limit that average longevity will approach but cannot exceed. If so, then survival beyond age 85 would not become increasingly likely for the average person, but would be limited to statistical outliers. The differing viewpoints deserve exploration in depth, not only because of the differences in survival projections they imply but also in their very different implications for rates of disability, chronic illness, and health care utilization by survivors.

Longer Survival for the Chronically Ill?

If the average age at death increases by more than the average age of onset of chronic illness, then the population suffering from chronic illness grows, giving rise to increases in dependency and resource use. Otherwise, the population grows older but healthier.[7] Thus, it is vital to understand the interdependence between chronic illness and death. Much is known about increases in adult longevity, but changes in morbidity are inherently more diverse and difficult to quantify than changes in mortality. This has left room for strikingly different interpretations of recent mortality and morbidity trends.

The simplest model of illness and death is one of independent competing risks. In that view, medical victories against life-threatening acute illnesses increase the prevalence of chronic illnesses, because they leave the age of onset of chronic conditions unaffected. This model seems most appropriate for the many chronic conditions whose risks of onset rise exponentially with age, termed "age-dependent" by Brody and Schneider (1986). Arthritis, for example, is age-dependent but has no apparent relation to life-threatening conditions, so that there is no reason to expect any delay in the onset of arthritis as longevity increases. Kramer (1980) projected stunningly rapid worldwide growth in mental disorders and chronic illness by the year 2000, assuming age-specific prevalence rates to be constant at levels observed in certain Western populations but allowing for expected population aging. He projected, for example, that cases of senile dementia in more developed countries would increase two-and-a-half times more rapidly than the total populations of those countries.

An even more pessimistic view is that acute and chronic illnesses are not independent; that, instead, the likelihood of acute illnesses is greatest for those weakened by chronic illness. If this is the case, then when we find a cure for a life-threatening acute illness, it is the chronically ill whose lives we are most likely to extend. Gruenberg (1977) argued that "our technological successes defy death's claim on the sick and the weak," so that our progress against the great killer diseases has been at the cost of prolonging the lives of those who are most ill. A prominent example is the steep decline in the death rate from pneumonia between 1936, when sulfa drugs were introduced, and the late 1940s. By preventing fatalities from pneumonia, medicine has tended to increase the average duration of other illnesses. Gruenberg lists mongolism, senile brain disease, arteriosclerosis, hypertension, schizophrenia, diabetes, and spina bifida as increasing in duration, and argues that we must recognize health technology to be a "great epidemiological force" in itself.

If the disabled are especially susceptible to life-threatening illnesses, then the argument applies equally well to disability (Feldman 1983). Improved survival for those afflicted with heart disease and other disabling ailments of late middle age can increase the prevalence of disability, even as it increases life expectancy. Thus, rising adult life expectancy does not by itself imply increasing vigor and self-sufficiency at older ages, so that longer lives do not necessarily translate into later retirement and reduced economic dependency.

Compression of Morbidity?

Fries (1980, 1983) has proposed a competing view of aging whose implications are quite opposite and altogether more optimistic with regard to morbidity and disability. The essence of his conceptual model is a recognition of aging itself as a cause of death which cannot be averted or delayed like other competing causes. Fries argues that there is for each individual at each age a genetically determined maximum physical capacity for each task the body must perform. These maximum capacities decline with age, and a personal history of more healthful living tends to bring actual capacity closer to the maximum for one's age. "Natural death" occurs when an organ is stressed beyond its capacity, so that the body can no longer maintain homeostasis, a state of physiological equilibrium. Kohn (1982) has argued that as many as 30% of deaths of elderly individuals may already be of this type, based on the observed absence of conditions that would be fatal to younger and more vital persons. According to Fries, the age at which the average body is no longer able to survive the stress of normal daily life is about 85, if that body is carefully maintained. This "life span" of 85, then, would be the limit that life expectancy would approach for the average person, due to secular improvements in healthful living, and this limit would be reached only in the absence of disease and accidents. Allowing for genetic heterogeneity, Fries asserts that life span has a range in the population of about ages 70–100.

Where others have argued that increases in longevity can exceed delays in chronic illness, Fries instead argues that by modifying known risk factors of major chronic illnesses, such as diet, smoking, and exercise, we can delay their onset and slow their progression, compressing the period of infirmity against a barrier of natural death. There is an ironic comfort in the claim of the inevitability of death, appealing as it does to our fears of frailty and dependence, and to our hope for life which is full and healthy to the end. In Fries's view, the most promising ways to improve the health of the aged are for insurers to avoid subsidizing bad health habits, and for aging policies to promote independence, through improved vocational opportunities and deinstitutionalization of necessary care.

Fries's vision of the decline of chronic illness is a very long-term view, as he freely acknowledges. For one thing, the effects of the aging of the 1945–1965 birth cohort on the average age of the population are likely to overwhelm any age-specific reduction in the prevalence of chronic illness for the next 50 years.

In addition, Fries predicts declines only in those conditions that are universal and progressive and have clinical symptom thresholds, multifactoral causes, and early onsets; he acknowledges that there are a few chronic illnesses, such as multiple sclerosis, rheumatoid arthritis, and Hodgkin's disease, whose courses cannot be greatly altered by lifestyle changes. In addition, we know that many progressive conditions, such as cancer, still contribute greatly to mortality in advance of any natural limit to life; delaying their progression will continue to increase their rate of incidence in the population by increasing their average duration, until they have been slowed to the point that most sufferers survive the disease and succumb instead to natural death. Fries asserts, nevertheless, that the ages at which clinical thresholds of lung cancer and heart attack are reached may be rising faster than life expectancy at 40, and, from clinical observation, that as many as one-fourth of deaths already occur within a few months of the decedents' ultimate physiological limits.

Fries (1983) presents a diverse set of arguments and body of evidence in favor of his model of natural death:

1. "Gompertz's Law," whereby mortality increases exponentially with age, provides a good fit to adult mortality rates, taken as a whole, but this rule also implies that survival becomes virtually impossible beyond a certain age.

2. The capacity of individual organs to sustain life appears, from clinical observation, to decline linearly with age. This linearity can be reconciled with the exponential change embodied in Gompertz's Law, if we recognize that many organs are subject to random daily perturbations in stress and that the failure of a single organ is sufficient to cause death.

3. The secular trend for "survival curves" (graphs that plot the survivors of a birth cohort against their age; see figure 2.2) is to plunge ever more steeply toward the abscissa between ages 80 and 90 with little apparent change in the right portion of the curve, which represents survival by the oldest old.

4. Death is virtually certain for all by age 110, regardless of individual variations in lifestyle, and this upper limit appears to have changed little in historical time.

5. There are obvious and undisputed genetically determined differences across species in longevity.

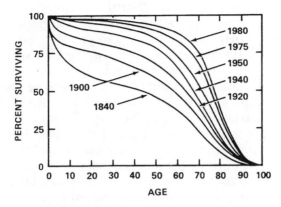

Figure 2.2 Rectangularization of U.S. survival curves
(from Fries and Crapo 1981, figure 1)

6. There are age-related bodily changes (such as graying of hair) which are not the result of disease.

7. The sizes of older cohorts always decline with age, indicating that the aging effect dominates any cohort effect on mortality.

8. Others, cited by Fries, have estimated past longevity from human fossil evidence, using an estimated relationship across species between the brain size/birth weight ratio and longevity, and have speculated that the human life span has not increased in 100,000 years.

The estimate of 85 as the average age of natural death arises from visual inspection of aggregate survival curves. The rate at which an individual's chance of survival declines with age is actually understated by aggregate survival curves, however, as long as the population is heterogeneous with respect to longevity (Manton 1982). In that case, as the population of survivors declined, they would be increasingly selected according to their exceptional longevity. Thus, even if every individual suffered rapid homeostatic deterioration in a narrow and genetically predetermined age range, the resulting population mortality rates would increase with age at a more gradual rate. The clinical findings of linear declines in organ reserve that Fries cites may be subject to the same selection bias, making those declines also more gradual in aggregate than they are for individuals. This all suggests that health deteriorates even more abruptly than Fries originally inferred from aggregate data, and observing the right-hand tails of aggregate survival curves can actually lead to overestimation of the average life span.

If natural death exists, then forecasts of aged populations that use widely accepted methods are likely to be greatly overestimated. Population projections like those produced by the Census Bureau (and the Social Security Administration, which refers to Census Bureau population projections in making its own financial projections) have historically used extrapolation methods: future mortality has generally been forecast to decline at a rate consistent with the declines experienced most recently (Olshansky 1988). A more formal approach to projection, the "cause-elimination" approach, projects the mortality gains from eliminating certain competing causes of death, and would tend to project slower declines in mortality. This is because the growing set of mortality threats, as a population ages, implies diminishing returns to the elimination of individual illnesses. But cause-elimination models include no hazard function for natural death, since mortality records do not allow for its inclusion as a cause of death. Like official extrapolations of past trends, cause-elimination models imply survival curves that are always shifting rightward, even at the oldest ages. If there is a genetically determined life span, as Fries has asserted, then both extrapolation methods and cause-elimination models will overpredict survival for the over-85 population in the mid-twenty-first century. Fries estimates that his model is consistent with a life expectancy at 85 as much as two years shorter by 2020 than the government projects. A difference of as much as two years is of great significance because of the very high rates of hospital and long-term-care utilization in the 85 and older age group.

Fries's critics (Manton 1982; Schneider and Brody 1983; Myers and Manton 1984) have subjected his hypothesis of a genetically limited life span to a barrage of empirical counterevidence and methodological criticisms. For one thing, even if as many as 30% of elderly deaths may arguably fit the pattern, the natural death described by Fries would still be the exception, with mortality at extreme ages typically characterized by a multiplicity of chronic degenerative diseases. And visual inferences from converging survival curves are suspect for several reasons. First, the shifts that took place in the early twentieth century were due primarily to reductions in mortality at the youngest ages, mortality that has largely been eliminated, so that a long-run tendency to square the survival curve tells us little about contemporary mortality trends. Further, the apparent squaring at older ages in previous decades was due in part to the use of abridged life tables which combine deaths above a fixed terminal age into an upper interval, such as 85 or older, obscuring the details of mortality improvements above that age. Nor does Gompertz's Law provide a very good fit to mortality rates at the oldest ages: the exponential rise in age-specific mortality rates actually gives way to a flattening at about age 100.

Survival curves did not in fact become squarer in the 1970s, and longevity did not behave as if it was approaching an absolute limit: there were substantial increases in survival at every age beyond about age 55, gains generally attributed to recent advances in the treatment of chronic disease, especially cardiovascular and cerebrovascular illnesses. And the longest-lived subpopulations tended to experience the greatest mortality improvements in the 1970s, contrary to the notion of a common upper limit to longevity. Mortality rates of those over age 85 fell

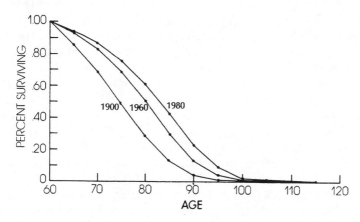

Figure 2.3 Survival curves for U.S. females alive at age 60
(from Myers and Manton 1984, figure 2)

faster than for other age groups, and mortality rates of women aged 65 and older decreased by more than men's, by a greater proportion in fact than those of women aged 55–64. Figure 2.3, a plot of survival curves of women alive at age 60, shows very broad-based mortality improvements since 1900, and little tendency toward squaring. In fact, the life expectancy of white women who had already reached Fries's proposed life span of 85 years increased by approximately two full years between 1960 and 1978. Survival beyond age 85 does not directly contradict Fries's hypothesis, because he allows for individual variation in life span; but this increase in life expectancy is extraordinarily large for a subgroup whose typical member should already have been within a few years of her maximum obtainable age.

More recently, however, mortality trends may have reversed. According to life tables published by the U.S. Public Health Service, the life expectancy of 85-year-olds peaked in 1982 (incidentally, just before the introduction of Medicare's prospective payment system) and declined between 1982 and 1988, as figure 2.4 shows. The divergence between female and male life expectancies has also ceased since 1982; in fact, there has been a slight convergence at most older ages, as figure 2.5 illustrates for 65-year-olds. Far from settling the controversy over the squaring of the survival curve, these recent data highlight the difficulty of settling the issue on the basis of a short recent time series. In any case, it would be entirely possible for men's and women's average life spans to be genetically determined but different, just as certain other gender-linked traits such as anatomical differences are genetically determined.

If morbidity is being compressed, then we should observe its onset and progression to be delayed by more than the age of death. At present there is disagreement whether morbidity is being delayed at all, or equivalently whether age-specific rates of morbidity are declining at all. Verbrugge (1984) examined changes in self-reported general health, disability, and prevalence of specific conditions in the 1960s and 1970s for middle-aged and older Americans. She found little trend in general health but increasing rates of morbidity from most of the leading nonfatal conditions and fatal diseases, even as mortality from most of the latter has declined. Respondents also reported increasing activity limitations per medically defined condition,

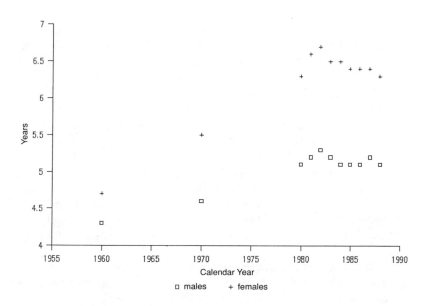

Figure 2.4 Remaining expectation of life, U.S. whites, age 85

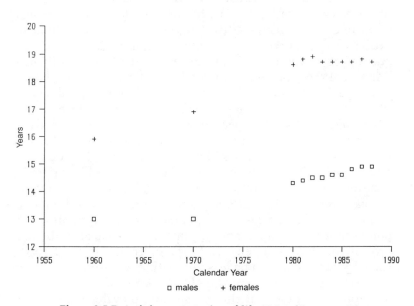

Figure 2.5 Remaining expectation of life, U.S. whites, age 65

primarily in the form of disability days spent out of bed. She attributed the increased morbidity and disability to earlier diagnosis and accommodation and to reduced mortality among those afflicted.

Verbrugge's study suffered, however, from the use of only two very broad age categories (45–64 and 65 +), and aging of the population within each of these age categories may account for some of the worsening of health that she observes. Palmore's (1986) analysis of trends in the same national survey led to conclusions opposite to Verbrugge's. Considering a broader set of self-reported health and disability measures, he found that some measures had upward and some downward trends for those aged 65 or older, but these measures had consistently decreased for the elderly, relative to their trends for the total population.

Manton has conducted several studies of specific major illnesses which indicate declining age-specific morbidity from those illnesses. In one such study (Manton 1982), he found that the major chronic diseases which declined in the 1970s as contributing causes of death seemed also to decline in severity for the surviving population. The frequency with which they were mentioned as underlying (that is, secondary but contributing) causes on death certificates declined just as rapidly as their frequency of citation as major causes. And in an examination (Manton 1986a) of data from death certificates for those dying after age 85, he found similar results. Looking at subpopulations ultimately dying of one of three major conditions associated with frailty, the expectation of age at death increased during the 1970s in each group (and generally by more than for those who died of primary killers such as cancer, heart disease, and stroke). Of the three conditions associated with frailty, pneumonia and hip fracture decreased in frequency as underlying causes of death, while septicemia increased in frequency but no more rapidly among this oldest old group than for the population as a whole. The implication is that mortality improvements have not selectively spared the frailest elderly, for the survivors appear to be less vulnerable to mortality from debilitating conditions than the elderly who came before them. Manton also notes that the age-specific prevalence of institutionalization appears not to be rising, despite increases in life expectancy at older ages.

A more recent review by Fries (1989) finds similar results with respect to heart disease, lung cancer, and automobile accidents, all of which rank among the major contemporary causes of death. In each case, he finds that most recent progress has been in the form of delayed onset rather than improved survival after onset.

Restrained Optimism: Morbidity as a Function of Years until Death

All of this argues against using constant age-specific rates of incidence to forecast the health care needs of tomorrow's growing elderly population: for now, the preponderance of evidence favors declining age-specific incidence. Fuchs (1984) has argued, in fact, that years until death is a much better predictor of health care utilization than years since birth, impending death being a more crucial determinant of medical needs than aging alone. Control for the time until death accounts, in fact, for much of the apparent effect of aging on utilization. Lubitz and Prihoda (1984), for example, estimated that 8% of Medicare expenditures in a recent year were incurred in the final 30 days of patients' lives, and 28% in the final year of life. They found Medicare reimbursements per enrollee year to be more than six times greater for those in their last year of life than for survivors, and more than half of the difference in reimbursements between youngest and oldest enrollees disappeared when they controlled for the different proportions of decedents in the two age groups.

This is cause for optimism regarding future health-care costs, because it implies that the postponement of death brings with it a postponement in the cost of dying. (More sobering, however, is the implication that significant reductions in per capita health-care spending may require cutting back on the care provided to the mortally ill.)

If Fuchs's implicit assumption is correct, that the age of onset of chronic illness is increasing at about the same rate as age at death, on average, then we can combine health and long-term-care utilization rates specific to years until death with mortality forecasts and make improved forecasts of total utilization. Roos, Montgomery, and Roos (1987) have done this for the Canadian Province of Manitoba, computing utilization rates by years-until-death. They found hospital utilization to be most concentrated in the years immediately prior to death, nursing home care[8] somewhat less so, and physician visits to increase only slightly with the approach of death. This compression of usage into the final years of life was itself a function of age, being greater for those surviving to older ages. Thus, in their cross-section sample, morbidity seemed generally to be compressed into the shortest period for those who lived the longest, the pattern forecast by Fries's model. Controlling for age until death greatly reduced the observed effect of age on hospital utilization. In fact, in the year prior to death, the year in which decedents spent the majority of their hospital days, utilization was not systematically higher for older patients. Ambulatory physician visits actually tended to decrease with age, after controlling for years until death. Age had a strong and positive independent effect, however, on nursing home use. Taken together, these findings suggest that hospital cost projections are most likely to be exaggerated by using constant age-specific utilization rates, while similar projections of nursing home and ambulatory costs are likely to be more reliable.

Not all of those who are in their last years of life are intensive users of care: sudden death may preempt the possibility of care. Roos, Montgomery, and Roos found that 35% of their study population spent less than 14 days in institutions during the final year of their lives, and heart attack victims were more likely than other decedents to fit this pattern. Similarly, Lubitz and Prihoda found that 8% of decedents had no Medicare reimbursements at all in their final year of life, while others used vastly more care than average, so that 13% of decedents accounted for 45% of reimbursements. With such a high degree of variation and skewedness in the use of services, even among those who are in the last year of life, models of morbidity and mortality must clearly be able to do more than simply explain trends in aggregate rates; they must faithfully model the interactions between numerous specific conditions and death.

More Recent Models of Aging and Death

What is at issue in the competing models described above, and what leads to very different predictions of the disabled and chronically ill populations, is the role that aging itself plays in producing sickness and death. In Gruenberg's view it is the age of onset and the rate of progression of debilitating disease that are most closely and unalterably age related: while causes of death can be eliminated, age-specific risks of chronic illness, conditional on survival, are invariant. In this case, the successful treatment of acute illness increases the prevalence of chronic illness. For Fries, on the other hand, it is the maximum ability to survive at each age that is unalterable, as determined by a fixed relation between age and maximum organ reserve. If organ reserve could be increased through changes in lifestyle and other risk factors, then the incidence of chronic illness could be reduced within a fixed life span.

Gruenberg's view is akin to the "cause-elimination" models described above: the elimination of a killer disease leaves a population still vulnerable to crippling conditions. Much of the progress against mortality in recent decades, however, was due to delays in the progress of chronic illnesses such as heart disease, through improvements in their management rather than due to reductions in the age-specific risk of onset. An additional unsatisfactory aspect of cause-elimination models is what they imply in the limit: as one cause of death after another is eliminated, we should observe the life span to be approaching immortality.

Instead of treating illness and death as determined by distinct processes, choosing one or the other to be more closely tied to aging, more recent modeling efforts have attempted to better integrate the mortality and morbidity effects of aging, and in so doing to address some of the failings outlined above. One such approach is the "cause-delay" model, in which causes of death are delayed rather than eliminated. In a demonstration of this approach, Olshansky (1985) examined the effect of a five-year delay in mortality from certain selected conditions by substituting for each age cohort the current mortality rate, from that condition, of the cohort that is younger by five years. The delayed risks retain the pattern of exponential increase with age, so that immortality is ruled out, and the model permits predictions of complex resulting changes in the prevalence of other age-related conditions as longevity increases.

This approach, unfortunately, risks confounding aging effects with vintage effects: the mortality rate of the younger cohort, intended to simulate delayed risks, may be lower because of the better general health associated with later vintage, in addition to any age advantage. Thus, the changes forecast by a cause-delay model are a mixture of two types, in unknown proportions: those that could occur naturally, as younger and healthier birth cohorts age, and those that may require new medical advances to delay the aging process. A snapshot of current mortality rates does not permit a decomposition of differences into these component vintage and aging effects. And while longitudinal data (time series of mortality rates by age) do in theory permit a decomposition, in practice the mortality rates of younger age cohorts from most illnesses are quite low. Substantial age and vintage-related differences in mortality do not emerge until rather late in life, so that data availability limits the time horizon for which cause-delay models can generate reliable forecasts.

Manton and Liu (1984) describe a promising approach to this problem, a "bioactuarial" illness-death model which explicitly represents the natural history of an individual chronic disease. Using cancer as an example, they model its onset, its progression beyond a clinical threshold, and death from the illness as transitions whose probabilities are functions of age and year of birth. For younger cohorts, there are richer data on numbers of clinically diagnosed cases than there are on deaths, so the inclusion of illness as an outcome permits more powerful estimation of cohort differences in susceptibility; differences between cohorts in mortality risks can then be derived from estimated differences in the risk of illness. And by explicitly modeling the relationship between observed clinical diagnosis and unobserved preclinical onset, the authors are able to estimate the prevalence in each age cohort of yet-undiagnosed illnesses.

Additional progress can be made by explicitly representing the process by which risks are delayed. Manton (1986b) has modeled risk factors, such as high blood pressure, as functions of age. He then modeled the age-specific risks of death from heart disease, cancer, and from other causes as separate functions, each the product of a multiplicatively interactive function of risk factors and an exponential function of age. In this way causes of death are allowed to be interdependent, and the reduction in a risk factor can reduce mortality from all causes of death simultaneously while leaving intact the property that death becomes virtually certain at some age.

An important implication of the more recent models described above is that disease need not be eliminated for substantial mortality improvement to occur. Instead, improvements in shared risk factors, such as reductions in smoking and blood cholesterol, can delay and greatly reduce population mortality. Olshansky (1985) estimates that a delay of five years in the risks associated with a set of major chronic illnesses has a comparable effect on life expectancy to the elimination of all cancers or all ischemic heart disease. And Manton (1986b) finds that complete control of known risk factors (such as to eliminate their increase with age and their person-to-person variation) could increase the remaining expectation of life at age 30 to about 57 years, about 10 years longer than its current value.[9]

At the same time, these models actually lead to downwardly revised estimates of the effect of disease elimination on mortality. Manton (1986b) finds that the effect on longevity of eliminating a single killer illness without a change in the underlying risk factor distribution would be less than in models with independent risks. Those with high risk factors for the full set of illnesses would be the ones most likely to be spared if a single illness were eliminated, leaving a population at increased risk, on average, for the remaining illnesses. This interdependence of competing risks would increase with age because averting deaths at younger ages would allow increased survival of high-risk people to older ages.

Rapid improvements in our understanding of the aging process will surely continue, because its current importance for population projection and health resource planning will make it a high-priority research area. The current evidence can be briefly summarized as follows: some chronic conditions are strictly age related and will become increasingly prevalent with mortality improvements. Greater longevity is nevertheless likely to be associated with delays in the progress of the major degenerative illnesses. And since the achievement of advanced age leaves one susceptible to increasing numbers of competing

causes of death, the increases in longevity that medical advances provide are likely to be smaller than they have been in
the recent past and to be increasingly difficult to achieve.

Needs and Burdens: Demography, Resource Use, and Economic Growth

Demographic Fluctuations and Economic Growth

The projected aging of the population raises this concern
above all others: Will an aging population create needs for
health and long-term care which are greater than our economy
can provide? Must society choose either a reduction in the
quality of care it provides to its younger members or some
other reduction in their living standard?

One measure of the standard of living that an economy can
provide is real Gross National Product (real GNP) per capita,
which is total production of goods and services per citizen
(whether working or dependent upon workers). Despite well-
known limitations,[10] GNP is quite suitable as a yardstick
against which to measure the projected demand for health and
long-term-care services.

Table 2.1 shows how GNP per capita has grown during selected intervals beginning in 1929. The steadiness of this
growth, when measured at intervals of a decade or longer, is
remarkable. Since 1950, the average annual growth rate of real
GNP per capita has never fallen below 1.5% for a decade or
risen above 2.5%. Even for the period 1929–1950, which included the Great Depression and the Second World War, the average growth rate of 1.5% was not much different from the
1.9% rate achieved during the succeeding 40 years, 1950–1990.

The growth rate of GNP per capita can be decomposed into
two parts, the growth rate of GNP per labor force member and
the growth rate of the labor force relative to the population.
(Note that the first column is the sum of the second and third
columns.) The labor force, which is defined as the sum of employed and unemployed people, is used here to examine the effects of demographic fluctuations and trends on production.
The labor force excludes children; this, and the smallness of
the birth cohort born in the 1930s, account for the decline in
the labor force relative to population during the Baby Boom

TABLE 2.1
Average Annual Growth Rates, Selected Intervals, 1929–1990 (%)

	GNP/Population	GNP/Labor Force	Labor Force/Population
1929–1950	1.5	1.4	0.1
1950–1960	1.5	2.1	−0.6
1960–1970	2.5	2.0	0.5
1970–1980	1.7	0.2	1.5
1980–1990	1.7	1.1	0.6
1950–1990	1.9	1.4	0.5

Source: Council of Economic Advisors (1991a, 1991b).
Note: GNP is measured in real terms, and only civilians are included in the Labor Force.

years 1950–1960. The labor force likewise excludes the retired, the disabled, and full-time homemakers. Since 1960, growing labor force withdrawals due to earlier retirement and increasing rates of disability have been more than offset by increases in female labor force participation and the coming of age of Baby Boomers; thus, the labor force has grown relative to population during those years. All in all, the growth rate of the labor force relative to population has fluctuated much more widely than the growth rate of GNP per capita, from a low of −0.6% in the 1950s to a high of 1.5% in the 1970s.

What has made the greater stability of GNP growth per capita possible has been offsetting variations in its other component, the growth of GNP relative to the labor force. In the 1950s, as families expanded, earnings per worker grew rapidly enough to support those families. As young workers flooded the labor market in the 1970s, GNP per worker stagnated; in the 1980s, labor force growth abated, while GNP growth rebounded.

An inverse relationship between labor force growth and GNP growth per labor force member is to be expected, because labor force growth tends to reduce the amount of capital per worker. Two types of capital are relevant. When the labor force grows, relative to population, it contains a growing proportion of untrained workers lacking "human capital." The amount of physical capital per worker also drops. For both of these reasons, the average productivity of workers tends to fall when the labor force rapidly expands and to rise when the labor force contracts.

Today, interest focuses on projected increases in the aged population and on declines in the numbers of new labor force entrants. Both factors will reduce the ratio of labor force to population: the Census Bureau (Spencer 1989) projects a decline at the rate of -0.1% per year between 1990 and 2040 in the fraction of the population aged 21–64. A continuing drop in the retirement age would make the decline in labor force per capita somewhat larger. If retirement ages declined by five years during the same period, this would contribute about another -0.3% to the annual rate of decline in labor force per capita.[11]

Nevertheless, the experience of the last 40 years, and especially of the 1950s, provides a basis for cautious optimism. When the growth rate of the labor force declines, productivity per worker appears to automatically increase, at least for periods as brief as a decade. Further increases in investment per worker could help to offset the coming sustained drop in the growth rate of the labor force, permitting GNP to continue to grow. In the next three decades, as Baby Boomers age and complete mortgage and child-rearing obligations, they will be in a position to rapidly accumulate retirement savings. The resulting increases in investment and productivity would boost GNP per worker, tending to offset the effects of the growing worker shortage on living standards.

The reasons for caution, however, are numerous. We can infer from table 2.1 that GNP growth per capita *can* be more stable than labor force growth per capita, not that it *must*, nor that the next 50 years must duplicate the previous 50. If we can promote productivity growth by promoting saving and investment, then we can make GNP growth per worker more rapid, but only the most optimistic would be content to let nature take its course, especially given the low U.S. saving rates of the 1980s.[12]

In addition, the mechanism for redistributing GNP from workers and owners of capital to older dependents is largely indirect and impersonal. Much of the income, health care, and long-term care provided to the elderly is transferred to them from the general public through the tax system and Social Security, Medicare, and Medicaid. Whereas parents in the 1950s readily used their rising per capita incomes to provide for their growing families, public transfers to the elderly assist other people's parents, not one's own, and therefore may be made less willingly. For this reason, increased saving by Baby Boomers is important not only for its effect on the earnings of the succeeding generation: the accumulated savings would also provide resources with which to meet retirement and health-care needs should workers balk at transferring sufficient funds through public programs.

The Economic Burden of Health Care and Long-Term Care

An aging population means growing demands for health and long-term care. By referring to the historical growth rates of GNP per capita in table 2.1, we are able to roughly gauge the economy's ability to meet those rising demands without sacrifice. Table 2.1 demonstrates that a growth rate below 1.5% for more than a period of a few years would be extraordinarily low by mid-twentieth-century standards. In a recent analysis of long-run demographic trends, the Office of the Actuary of the Health Care Financing Administration (HCFA) projected the rate of annual real GNP growth per capita to fall from 1.9% in 1990 to 1.1% by 2020 and then to rise to 1.6% by 2040, averaging about 1.4% over the entire period 1990–2040 (HCFA 1987).

Compared to those HCFA projections, or to the historical record of the past 60 years, a growth rate of 1% per year in per capita real GNP would be quite low. Yet, as table 2.2 shows, 1% annual growth may be more than sufficient to provide the increased physician and hospital services implied by the population aging expected in the next 50 years. The figures in table 2.2 are projections of the growth rates of the utilization of med-

TABLE 2.2
Projected Annual per Capita Growth Rates (%)

	1980–2000	2000–2020	2020–2040
Physician visits	0.06/0.02	0.09/0.03	0.05/0.02
Short stay hospital days	0.69/0.60	0.50/0.67	0.56/0.55
Nursing home residents	1.81/1.90	0.85/0.97	1.88/2.12
Number of persons with limitations in activities of daily living	1.00/—	0.83/—	1.10/—

Source: Rice and Feldman (1983); Health Care Financing Administration (1987).

ical and nursing home services. The first entry in each cell is adapted from Rice and Feldman (1983) and the second from the more recent set of projections produced by HCFA (1987). In each case, the method of construction was to assume constant utilization rates for each age and sex category, so that any projected growth is due entirely to assumed changes in the age distribution of the population.[13] Within each cell, the independently estimated growth rates are strikingly similar.

Visits to physicians are projected to increase least rapidly of the three utilization measures in table 2.2: this is because aging has a relatively small effect on the frequency of physician visits. A more rapid increase is projected for inpatient hospital days, since rates of hospitalization rise more rapidly with age. Finally, nursing home and disability populations are projected to grow most rapidly. This is because rates of disability and nursing home use increase exponentially with age: in each succeeding decade of life after age 65, the probabilities of disability and nursing home residency roughly double and triple, respectively, according to the survey findings used by Rice and Feldman in their projections. This is also why the nursing home and disabled populations are projected to grow especially rapidly in the years 2020–2040, the period in which all surviving Baby Boomers born before 1955 will reach 85 years of age.

In the light of demographic evidence reviewed above, we may ask whether the use of recent age-specific rates of utilization biases projections upward or downward. While we cannot lightly dismiss the contention that morbidity worsens as longevity increases, the weight of the still-accumulating evidence is in favor of declining age-specific morbidity. With new models of risk factors and complex mortality-morbidity interactions still in their infancy, the best available benchmark to use in assessing the bias in these projections is Fuchs's claim that remaining life expectancy is a more accurate predictor of morbidity and health care utilization than chronological age. Judging from the findings of Roos et al. (1987), it is the growth in inpatient hospital utilization that is most exaggerated by assuming fixed age-specific utilization rates, because this category of care is the most highly concentrated in the final year of life; they show projections of outpatient and nursing care to be affected very little by basing assumed utilization rates on years until death. Viewed in this light, the likely per capita growth rates of both inpatient and outpatient utilization are well below historical rates of per capita GNP growth; only the rate of growth of nursing home residents would be of the same order of magnitude as mid-twentieth-century GNP growth, and the former is projected to be particularly high in the period 2020–2040.

Even the projected rate of growth of nursing home residents will overshoot the target if Fries is correct in his claim that demographers have overprojected increases in life expectancy at age 85. While demographers generally dismissed his predictions in the early 1980s, subsequent life-expectancy data have been more supportive of Fries; if the trend were to continue, then nursing home residency would grow less rapidly than table 2.2 indicates.

In any case, the projections demonstrate that demographic changes alone are not sufficient cause for medical care expenditures to absorb an increasing share of GNP. There are, however, two other equally important potential causes of expenditure increases. First, the intensity of care per visit could increase for reasons other than aging, such as a change in the number and complexity of procedures performed during the average patient's visit. Second, the cost of a given amount of care would also increase if its price rose more rapidly than the general level of other prices in the economy. Since 1965, the intensity of medical care per incident has by itself generally increased more rapidly than GNP per capita, and medical inflation has also been greater than inflation in other prices (HCFA 1987). If these trends continue, then medical care will continue to consume an increasing share of GNP, but population aging will be at most a minor contributor to that phenomenon. And, in fact, third-party payers (Medicare and private insurers) have made progress in the late 1980s in slowing the growth of medical expenditures. More will be said about their efforts in Chapter 3.

There remains a final set of demographic trends affecting society's ability to provide care, and those are trends in family structure. Survivors need more institutional care than married people with healthy spouses, and so the rapid growth in the population of aged widows accounts for much of the growth in institutional care. In fact, Manton and Soldo (1985), using projection methods similar to the methods used to construct table 2.2, show more than half of the projected 1980–2040 increase in the nursing home population to be composed of women without spouses.

But they also project large increases in the noninstitutionalized disabled population, including substantial increases among married persons under age 85. This means that the burden of informal care, provided by spouses, offspring, and relatives, will rapidly increase at the same time that nursing home expenditures are expanding. And long-term trends in living arrangements are gradually making it more difficult for the impaired elderly to receive assistance from family members. Those trends, which are well documented elsewhere (e.g., Davis and Rowland 1986), include a decrease in children per parent, an increase in the proportion of elderly who live apart from their children, increased geographic distance between parents and children, an increase in the proportion of daughters who are employed, and a rapid increase in the proportion of elderly who live alone by reason of divorce. All of these factors tend to shift care from the family to more formal settings, and provision of services from in-kind to government-administered care.

The increasing role of public programs in providing care is probably the greatest destabilizing influence on our ability to provide for an aging population. The decline in the labor force relative to population in the 1950s produced little intergenerational tension, because the bulk of the expanding dependent population was made up of children, members of worker's households. But independent-living elderly in the twenty-first century will likely be viewed by workers as having a weaker claim on worker's incomes, especially to the extent that redistribution takes place through government transfers rather than through intrafamily gifts. Workers may balk at transferring an increasing share of income to others through taxes, regardless of the willingness of workers in earlier decades to devote a comparably large share to the care of immediate family members.

For this reason, rising tension over transfers between generations may be the greatest obstacle to providing adequate care for older people in the twenty-first century. Greater ownership of productive capital, through saving and investment, could lessen that tension, enabling older Americans to finance more of their own care. This could be brought about by expanding private medical and long-term-care insurance to meet growing needs, instead of putting all of the additional burdens of care for an aging population on tax and transfer programs. Long-term-care financing, in particular, has reached a crucial juncture: with families increasingly unable to provide services directly, greater institutionalization will require substantial increases in either public or private financing.

Much of the formal medical and long-term nursing care received by the elderly is now financed through government programs. Chapter 3 describes those programs and addresses the extent to which taxes and transfers will need to be increased if we follow the current course of healthcare and long-term-care financing into the first half of the next century.

3

Medical and Long-Term Care Today: Financing Problems and Gaps in Coverage

The Emerging Weakness of Pay-as-You-Go Financing

SINCE THE establishment of the Social Security program in 1935, the United States has continued to expand and strengthen its system of social insurance, a broad income-security safety net for workers and their families. Benefits for the unemployed, the disabled, the retired, survivors of deceased workers, and the aged in ill health are financed by payroll taxes and available to workers regardless of demonstrated need.

These programs are primarily financed on a "pay-as-you-go" basis: current tax revenues are used to pay current benefits, instead of being saved to fund future benefits, and the programs' trust funds have at most times been only large enough to weather unexpected temporary revenue shortfalls.

There can be very substantial advantages to choosing pay-as-you-go financing over full funding, and these advantages were evident in the 1930s and the three decades that followed. First, the pay-as-you-go scheme enables a new program to pay immediate benefits (such as retirement benefits) to those in need, without prior contributions. The program incurs a debt to workers, repaid through benefit payments to them at a later date, and financed by taxing the next cohort of workers. A new debt is thereby incurred to those workers, which is paid back by taxing the next cohort, and so on indefinitely. In essence, a pay-as-you-go system borrows from the distant future to pay benefits to an initial cohort of beneficiaries who have made little contribution of their own. During the Great Depression, with its bank failures and scarcity of employment for young and old, pay-as-you-go Social Security was an attractive way to

40

make retirement possible for those whose resources would otherwise have been inadequate, at the same time increasing the chance of employment for younger workers.

Second, the rapid economic and population growth of the mid-twentieth century has enabled subsequent generations of workers to prosper under pay-as-you-go systems: intergenerational transfers are expected to provide even those who are currently retiring with greater lifetime income than would have been provided by a funded system.[1] Today's labor force entrants nevertheless may ultimately receive less from transfers than from a funded system; optimal choices for each generation depend critically on growth trends during their lives.

It may be surprising that transfers through a pay-as-you-go program can earn a higher rate of return than contributions to a fully funded program, but pay-as-you-go actually outperforms saving as long as the payroll tax base grows sufficiently rapidly. Just as savings earn a return by being invested in productive capital, payroll tax contributions also can earn a positive return if each successive generation is able to make larger and larger transfers to its elders, for then each generation's benefits exceed its contributions.

The relationship between the return to saving and the return to pay-as-you-go contributions is easy to grasp in the context of the following simple model: suppose that the employed labor force grows at a constant rate n per generation, that real wages per worker grow at a steady rate w per generation, and that financial assets earn real interest at a constant rate r per generation. (The word "real," in each case, indicates measurement after controlling for price inflation.) Imagine also that the payroll tax rate, the percentage of earnings paid to finance social insurance, is held constant from generation to generation. Because the payroll tax base benefits from both wage and employment growth, it grows at a rate of $(w + n)$ per generation, so that revenues are always sufficient to provide each retired person with transfers equal to $(1 + w + n)$ times the tax paid a generation before. In contrast, a dollar committed by a worker to personal savings is transformed into $(1 + r)$ dollars, a generation later, regardless of changes in employment and wage growth rates. If n and w are sufficiently large, then $(1 + r)$ dollars are less than the $(1 + w + n)$ dollars which can be earned by committing the dollar to a tax-and-transfer scheme (Samuelson 1958; and Aaron 1966).[2]

The remarkable result is that, in a world with sufficiently high population growth, not just the first generation but all generations for all time can be made financially better off by instituting a system of intergenerational transfers, instead of permitting the same funds to be saved: all are winners, and there are no losers. Unlike pyramid schemes, which must collapse when the finite universe of potential participants is exhausted, each generation in an intergenerational transfer system is able to receive a return to its contributions because infinite time guarantees that there will always be succeeding generations. The process amounts to borrowing from the infinite future, and the fact that the infinite future is never quite attained, so that the debt is never really repaid, is the key to the possibility of costlessly improving the welfare of all. That possibility has been called the "Social Insurance Paradox."

But just the opposite is the case if population and wage growth rates are sufficiently small. Aside from the first (noncontributing) generation, which is made better off in any case, the institution of a permanent program of intergenerational transfers will impoverish each and every generation, relative to the saving of the same funds, if the payroll tax base grows too slowly. Instead of earning interest at rate r, contributions grow only at the lower rate $(w + n)$.

The current and projected low rate of growth of the working-age population has been documented in Chapter 2. The growth rate of employment has three major determinants. First and foremost, there is the rate of population growth, which has rapidly declined since the 1950s. Second, there are changes in the rates of employment of successive cohorts. While employment is subject to considerable short-term ups and downs, the most important long-term trends have been in labor force participation rates of women and of older men. Increases in the participation of women have been sufficient to increase the percentage of adults who are in the labor force from 60% in 1970 to 67% by 1989,[3] despite declines in the age of retirement which caused a substantial drop in the participation of 55–64-year-old men during the same period. Third, even when population and rates of employment are stable, the relevant employed population still grows if more and more sectors of the labor force (such as occupations) become covered by the program with each successive generation of workers. This was the case with Social Security, and expansions of coverage accounted for much of the mid-century growth in its tax base.

In recent years, numerous "moneys-worth" analyses have been conducted concerning the largest intergenerational transfer, namely Social Security, and private saving. These often compare a representative worker's lifetime treatment by Social Security with the alternative of private saving. As we have seen, the outcome depends primarily on the underlying assumptions about wages, population growth, and interest rates, that is, whether $(w + n)$ will be less than r in the future. A very prominent analyst, long-time Social Security chief actuary Robert Myers (1985), has concluded that Social Security may be "a poor bargain for young new entrants when the combined employer-employee tax is considered." (Employers must match their employees' payroll tax payments, and employees in effect may be forced to pay much of this employer contribution through wage reductions.) Based on his estimates, the combined taxes paid over the lifetime of a young mid-1980s career entrant, accumulated with interest, will equal about 1.5 times the lifetime benefits that will be paid to that worker, and may ultimately be close to two times lifetime benefits for later birth cohorts. Others producing results similarly unfavorable to intergenerational transfers include Boskin et al. (1983, 1987), Boskin (1986), and Pellechio and Goodfellow (1983). Of course, future real interest rates cannot be treated as known constants, any more than wages and population growth can. Boskin et al. (1987) assume in their central projections that workers can earn 3% real interest on their savings, but a change to a real interest rate of 2% improves the relative performance of pay-as-you-go. At 2% interest, certain Baby Boomers who are relatively favored by Social Security's benefit formula would become wealthier from a transfer scheme than from saving, namely, single-earner couples who are at or below median incomes.

Just as future interest rates are not known constants, there will of course be variations in the actual rates of return earned by different individuals and families on their savings. Nevertheless, the message from the studies cited above is that the typical family is likely to receive less in future decades from pay-as-you-go programs than from interest on their savings, if the real interest rate that they earn remains in the historical range of 2%-3%. Boskin et al. (1987) provide useful break-even estimates for Baby Boom couples with roughly median earnings ($40,000 in 1985). They project that one-earner couples with those earnings will receive benefits (including the non-contributory spouse's benefit) from Social Security providing the equivalent of 2.07% real interest. For two-earner couples with the same earnings, they estimate the rate of return to Social Security contributions to be only 1.22%, there being no spouse's benefit in this case. If these figures are correct, real interest rates would have to be very low by historical standards for even half of Baby Boomer couples to be as well served by pay-as-you-go as by an alternative savings scheme.

Thus, slow growth in the payroll tax base has apparently turned the rate of return advantage of pay-as-you-go programs upside-down. This makes the 1990s and the early twenty-first century a poor time to undertake new pay-as-you-go programs or expansions of existing ones. While much of this discussion has been framed in terms of the Social Security retirement program, the reasoning applies equally well to Medicare and Medicaid as providers of medical and long-term-care services to the aged. Each is financed primarily by taxes paid by workers, so each consists largely of intergenerational transfers. And comparisons between intergenerational transfers and savings actually can be more broadly applied than to pay-as-you-go social insurance programs alone: they apply not only to transfers made through the public sector but also to private transfers. The latter occur whenever children care and provide financially or otherwise for their own parents, and the arithmetic of low population growth is just as unfavorable to private transfers as it is to public transfers.

Thus, we approach the next century with a demographic environment that appears to favor saving and with a system of social insurance heavily dependent on intergenerational transfers. This conflict threatens the very existence of the public programs which today finance health and long-term care for the aged.

Medical Care: Medicare Coverage and Financing

Coverage

Medicare provides medical insurance to almost all older Americans: of the 31.0 million persons aged 65 or older in 1989, 29.9 million were enrolled in Hospital Insurance (HI), the portion of Medicare that pays for hospital expenses, and 29.2 million were enrolled in Supplementary Medical Insurance (SMI), the portion that pays physicians' fees.[4] Both programs also provide benefits to the younger disabled, but that group makes up less than 10% of the enrollment of either program.[5]

Entitlement to HI benefits is automatic when one becomes entitled to Social Security retirement benefits; Social Security entitlement is in turn acquired by working in covered employment and paying payroll taxes for 40 calendar quarters. There is no automatic entitlement to SMI, but neither are calendar quarters of past covered employment required: any persons aged 65 or older may elect to enroll in SMI by paying a premium. HI is also available to those without automatic entitlement as long as they enroll in SMI and pay an additional HI premium. Any surplus revenues of HI and SMI are kept in separate trust funds, where they are invested in U.S. government securities.

The creation of Medicare in 1965 vastly improved the medical coverage of the elderly. Only a few years before, a survey of Social Security beneficiaries had revealed that only 29% had insurance for hospitalization and surgery, with an additional 15% insured for hospitalization only. Coverage was sparsest at the oldest ages: of those 80 years of age or older, for example, only 16% were covered for hospitalization and surgery, and 11% for hospitalization only (Bureau of Old Age and Survivors Insurance 1959).

Nevertheless, sizable gaps in coverage remain: while Medicare is generous in its coverage of acute episodes requiring hospitalization, it is less generous in its coverage of routine care for chronic conditions. For example, in a 1980 study of the elderly, those who were hospitalized paid for only 18% of their health-care costs out-of-pocket, while those who were neither hospitalized or admitted to any other institutions paid for 68% of costs out-of-pocket (Kovar 1986).

Coverage under Medicare's HI portion is most complete for stays of 60 days or less. HI covers a wide range of inpatient hospital services subject to a single $652 "first-day" deductible. A daily coinsurance amount of $163 applies to each subsequent day up to the ninetieth day, and a single "lifetime reserve" of 60 additional days of coverage is available thereafter, subject to $326 daily coinsurance. (All of these are 1992 dollar amounts, and all are increased each year at the same rate as HI hospital reimbursements.) Beyond 150 days, hospital expenses are no longer reimbursible by HI.

Along with inpatient services, HI covers related care supplied by skilled nursing facilities, for up to 100 days per spell of illness, and by home health agencies, on an intermittent basis: "intermittent" is defined as up to four days per week or up to 21 consecutive eight-hour days if medically necessary. The care must in each case be skilled and must be certified by a physician as necessary to rehabilitation from an acute illness. Stays in skilled nursing facilities are covered only if preceded by a three-day hospital stay. Patients in skilled nursing facilities pay no coinsurance for the first 20 days of care and currently pay $81.50 per day (in 1992) for each subsequent day. HI also covers membership in Health Maintenance Organizations (HMOs), provided that they offer the full package of benefits provided by Medicare and charge no more than the rate that the general public would be charged for the same coverage. Enthoven (1987) speculates that the HMO's advantages of low cost, little paperwork, financial predictability, and comprehensive services make it "likely to become the health care delivery system of choice for most Medicare beneficiaries."

SMI covers physicians' services, related health services, and supplies furnished by physicians and by hospital outpatient facilities. All are subject to a $100 annual deductible and require 20% copayment. Patients whose physicians charge fees in excess of SMI's approved fee scale (about 19% of claims in 1990)[6] also must pay the excess out of pocket. Thus, cost-sharing is typically greater for physicians' fees than for hospital fees, and with no ceiling on the 20% copayment, out-of-pocket costs can be catastrophically high for the most seriously ill.

Although the vast majority of Medicare reimbursement dollars go for care delivered in institutional settings, home health-care coverage has increased in recent years, as the role of Title XX of the Social Security Act has gradually diminished. The latter, since its implementation in 1974, has paid for much of the home and community services provided for the elderly. It provides block grants to the individual states and allows them wide flexibility in their choice of services, but its annual budget has been capped at about $2.5 billion since shortly after its passage. Medicare's contribution to community-based care has grown since 1972, when SMI's 20% coinsurance requirement was dropped for home- and community-based care, and when experimental waivers of HI institutionalization requirements were first authorized. Although the cost-effectiveness of home care has not been conclusively demonstrated by those experiments (Hughes 1986), HI's maximum number of home visits and prior hospitalization requirement were dropped in 1980. Another large increase in Medicare home health visits resulted, since SMI had required a deductible but HI did not. Almost all home health reimbursements are now made by HI rather than SMI, as the law requires when coverage overlaps.

Additional catastrophic medical coverage was added to Medicare in 1988 but repealed in 1989: it would have picked up HI's coinsurance payments after the initial deductible, imposed a ceiling of $1,320 on SMI out-of-pocket costs, and would also have paid 80% of the cost of filling outpatient drug prescriptions, above a deductible. The coverage would have been mandatory for Medicare enrollees, each of whom would have been required to pay an additional premium and a surcharge on federal income taxes. Funds for catastrophic care would have flowed through a new and separate trust fund, and premiums would have been automatically adjusted by a formula designed to keep reserves at about 20% of annual outlays.

This catastrophic coverage would have been the only portion of Medicare to be entirely paid for by its enrolled population. The federal income tax surcharge would, in addition, have made this the most redistributive part of the program with respect to incomes. This, and the fact that more affluent enrollees typically have private supplementary health insurance, which would have overlapped considerably with the new catastrophic coverage, made the higher-income elderly a vocal constituency for the 1989 repeal of this additional coverage.

Revenues

The HI payroll tax paid by both employer and employee was only 0.6% of taxable earnings until 1972 and remained below 1.0% until 1978, but the rate is now 1.45%. This is about one-fifth of the combined 7.65% payroll tax for the combined Social Security programs, which include HI and Old Age, Survivors, and Disability Insurance (OASDI). Almost all of HI's revenues come from payroll taxes, although trust fund interest provides a small amount (about 11% in 1990) of total revenue. HI premiums from voluntary enrollees are an insignificantly small revenue source.[7]

Congress adjusts HI and other federal payroll tax rates infrequently in such a way as to strive for financial balance over a career-length period. In contrast, SMI premiums are adjusted annually to meet the year's projected expenditures, and they pay only a portion of the program's costs, the remainder being appropriated from general funds. The cost-sharing in SMI between premiums and general revenues was an even split for the first years of the program, but by late 1983 general revenues contributed $3.43 for every dollar in premiums paid by aged enrollees.[8] Premiums had begun to fall behind general revenues in 1972, when Congress placed a ceiling on the rate of growth of premiums equal to the rate of each year's cost-of-living adjustments in Social Security. This limited increases in premiums to an average of about 8% per year over the period 1972–1983; in contrast, prices of medical care services rose at a rate of about 10% per year over the same period.[9] Since 1983, Congress has required premiums to cover one-fourth of SMI costs for enrollees aged 65 and older.

HI Financial Projections

The HI payroll tax rate is currently scheduled to remain at 1.45%, for employer and employee each, indefinitely. While this tax rate has been adequate to accumulate growing HI reserves since 1983, it is expected to be too low to provide a fund for the mid-twenty-first century. Under intermediate projections made by HI's actuaries, the program's annual costs will rise above its scheduled tax revenues in the mid-1990s and will be more than double its revenues by 2020 (Board of Trustees of HI Trust Fund 1991). Figure 3.1 shows this by comparing tax

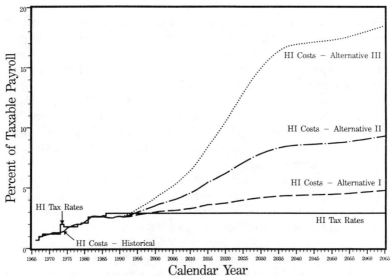

Note: HI projected costs shown are expenditures attributable to insured beneficiaries only, on an incurred basis, without an allowance for maintaining the trust fund balance at a desired level.

Figure 3.1 Estimated HI costs and tax rates (from Trustees of HI Trust Fund 1991, figure 3)

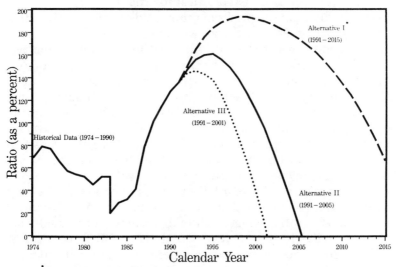

*The trust fund is depleted in 2018 under alternative I.

Note: The trust fund ratio is defined as the ratio of assets at the beginning of the year to disbursements during the year.

Figure 3.2 Short-term HI Trust Fund ratios (from Trustees of HI Trust Fund 1991, figure 1)

revenues and costs, each measured as a percentage of taxable payroll: alternative II is the intermediate projection. A comparison that uses GNP as a base may be easier to interpret, since taxable payroll is affected by trends in fringe benefits: whereas HI now costs about 1.2% of GNP, its cost would rise to about 2.7% of GNP by 2020, and 3.6% by 2040.[10] The HI fund would, in fact, be exhausted and, therefore, unable to make timely disbursements by about 2005, as figure 3.2 shows. The economic and demographic assumptions underlying the intermediate projections merit closer scrutiny.

These projections are much gloomier than those presented in table 2 of Chapter 2, and yet the two sets of projections are based on very similar demographic assumptions. In this sense, the financial problems forecast by HI's actuaries cannot be attributed to demographic forces alone. The additional factor which must be taken into account is medical cost inflation.

The Rice and Feldman and HCFA projections presented in Chapter 2 were of growth rates of medical and nursing care utilization (for example, number of patient days), not of expenditures. To assume real expenditures to grow at the same rate as utilization implicitly treats the real cost of each type of medical and nursing care as constant, meaning that their prices rise no more rapidly than the prices of other goods and services; in this case, we have seen that the growth rates of hospital and physician expenditures, based on projected demographic changes, would be lower than any recent historical growth rates of GNP. But to treat the real cost of a hospital stay as constant is to deny the possibility of increasingly intensive or high-quality care, even as rising real wages increase real per capita consumption of other goods and services. Nor does it allow for above-average inflation for any other reason, even though the rate of hospital cost inflation has been as high as, or higher than, the overall inflation rate in every year but one since 1970.[11]

In contrast, the 75-year HI actuarial projection allows for a continuation of higher-than-average inflation in its assumed inpatient cost inflation rate: while this rate would gradually decline over the initial 25-year period (1991–2015), continuing HI's recent success at cost containment, it would still equal the rate of wage (not price) inflation over the final 50 years (2016–2065).[12] This would allow the quality of reimbursed care, taking into account its intensity per visit, to increase at about the same rate as the average standard of living, since the excess of wage inflation over price inflation measures the improvement in the average earner's purchasing power. Wage-related increases in benefits have precedent in our long-range Social Security retirement policy: Social Security's benefit formula guarantees that retirement benefit levels increase, generation-by-generation, according to increases in wage levels, and this permits retirement benefits to keep pace with the wages that they are replacing. In the same way, HI's actuarial projections assume that the services consumed per hospital stay would grow as rapidly as other components of the average standard of living.[13]

Under these circumstances, increases in the number of enrollees per worker must increase expenditures relative to payroll: figure 3.1 shows the result. The intermediate projections assume that, between 2010 and 2035, the ratio of the population aged 65 and over to the population aged 20–64 increases from 0.22 to 0.38, causing costs to grow much faster than taxable payroll. The demographic shift is then assumed to stabilize in the third and final 25-year period of the projection. Before 2040, the youngest of the baby boom cohort will reach age 65, so the growth of costs will slow dramatically relative to payroll, as figure 3.1 shows. The intermediate projections also assume that fertility per woman will remain near its current level indefinitely, stabilizing at 1.9 children per woman, and they extrapolate mortality improvements gradually downward from the trajectory observed since 1968.[14] Mortality extrapolations like the latter have not proven very reliable as elements of past actuarial assumptions sets (Olshansky 1988). They have generally underpredicted the rapid increases in life expectancy that have occurred since 1975.

What we learn from the HI financial projections is that the program is very likely to require an infusion of new funds in order to continue operations beyond the early years of the twenty-first century. Unless we can suppress hospital cost inflation to a rate sufficiently below the growth rate of wages, in part by limiting improvements in the quality and intensity of care, taxable payroll cannot keep up with the medical expenditures of an aging population.

The HI projections also include optimistic and pessimistic alternatives, and the optimistic and pessimistic assumption sets differ most from the intermediate set for the 25-year period 1991–2015. Both alternative sets assume the growth of costs to gradually converge during the second 25-year period to the growth rate assumed for the intermediate case. The optimistic and pessimistic HI projections actually assume approximately the same growth of expenditures relative to payroll as the intermediate assumptions, beyond 2040; thus, none of the projections really make any allowance for optimism or pessimism with regard to events occurring after 2040.[15] This accounts for the parallel trajectories beyond that date in figure 3.1.

Even the optimistic projection indicates a need for substantial tax increases or other changes within 25 years. The assumptions behind this projection include hospital cost controls which are so successful, possibly due to further legislative tightening of reimbursement limits, that the average growth rate of HI expenditures relative to payroll between 1991 and 2015 would be less than half that assumed in the intermediate projection. This projected slow growth in spending is also due in part to an assumption that life expectancy at age 65 will increase by much less in the first 25 years of the forecast than it did in the preceding 10.[16] Even with this auspicious launching point from which to begin the baby boom's retirement, the subsequent expected demographic shift would still leave HI's budget short by about 1.6% of payroll in each year after 2040.[17] And under the pessimistic assumptions, in which life expectancy at 65 is about 2.5 years greater by 2015 than it is today, HI's costs in that year would already be about triple the revenues generated by its currently scheduled payroll tax.

In summary, substantial increases in tax rates are likely to be necessary, under current pay-as-you-go financing arrangements, in order to allow medical care for the aged to improve at the same rate as other aspects of twenty-first century living standards. Barring tax increases, the resources available to finance medical care can grow more rapidly than taxable payroll only if Baby Boomers increase the rate at which they set aside savings to fund their future health care expenditures, through increased advance funding of either public programs or private insurance.

SMI Financial Projections

Because SMI is funded on an accrual basis, like yearly renewable term insurance, its trustees do not report long-term financial projections. Instead, changes in expenditures are monitored annually, and general revenue appropriations and premiums are automatically adjusted to meet them. Nevertheless, the finances of SMI are subject to the same economic and demographic trends as HI, and until 1983 the expenditures of the two programs grew roughly in tandem, with SMI expenditures staying at about 40% of HI spending. Since 1983, SMI has been less successful than HI in lowering the rate of growth of its costs, and SMI costs rose to 66% of that of HI by 1990.[18]

Even if the future growth of SMI costs can be held to the rate projected for HI costs under intermediate assumptions, the cost of SMI will rise by the year 2035 to the rough equivalent of a pair of 2.7% payroll taxes, on both employers and employees. (Of course, this burden would be borne by beneficiary premiums and by all who pay individual and corporate income taxes, not by payroll taxes.) In all, the combined burden of financing Medicare's two parts would rise to about 14% of taxable payroll, from about 4% today.[19]

Competition with Social Security for Funds

To make matters worse, the other portions of Social Security (Old Age, Survivors, and Disability Insurance or OASDI) will also need to find some new revenues by about 2020; they already compete with HI by taxing payroll, and with SMI by taxing the incomes of the higher-income elderly. OASDI, whose total budget dwarfs that of Medicare, is projected under intermediate assumptions to be in close actuarial balance for the period 1991–2047, with annual surpluses expected for the first 27 years and annual deficits thereafter. But subsequent underfunding, under intermediate assumptions, leaves OASDI out of close actuarial balance over the customary 75-year valuation period (1991–2065), with revenues equal to only 92.4% of costs over that full time span. And the long-range prospects for OASDI are really worse for several reasons.

First, it is quite possible that the taxation of OASDI benefits will be repealed or scaled down sometime in the next few decades. This provision of the law was an essential component of the reform package which restored Social Security's solvency in 1983. It makes one-half of Social Security retirement benefits subject to personal income taxation for the high-income elderly, defined as individuals whose incomes exceed $25,000 and couples with incomes exceeding $32,000, and the revenues are returned to the OASDI trust funds. The income cutoff exempts all but those in the upper tail of the income distribution, and a cutoff was certainly necessary to make the change politically possible. What was not well known in 1983, however, is that the income cutoffs are fixed in nominal terms, not price- or wage-indexed like most other parameters of the Social Security benefit structure, so that an ever-increasing fraction of benefits will be taxed each year. In fact, if the cost of living continues to rise at an average rate of 4% per year, as it has in the late 1980s, then by 2024 the official U.S. poverty threshold for couples will have risen above the $32,000 cutoff, so that virtually all beneficiaries who pay income taxes will see their benefits taxed. As the public awakens to the full extent of Social Security's authority to take back a portion of benefit payments, it may demand repeal. But without the taxation of benefits, OASDI would need to increase its revenues by about 0.7% of payroll in order to restore the income lost between now and 2065.[20]

Even if that repeal does not occur, we should expect the financial projections to gradually deteriorate. The reason for this is that we officially evaluate trust fund adequacy over a closed 75-year interval, and the interval used for current projections includes large annual deficits in its final years. (See figure 3.3, in which I, II, and III again indicate optimistic, intermediate, and pessimistic scenarios, respectively.) Thus, even if the OASDI programs were in exact 75-year actuarial balance, their trust funds would be exhausted in 2065 and austerity measures would be necessary to continue operations thereafter. This underfunding on the distant horizon worsens the long-run projections a little more every year, because each year's passage brings a new year of shortfall into the 75-year forecast interval. Barring unexpected events, the long-run OASDI budget will be substantially out of balance by 2010, as the vanguard of the baby boom begins to retire. So just as problems financing medical and long-term care become most severe, Congress is likely

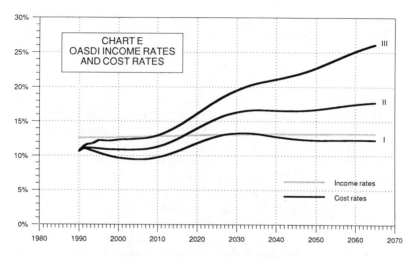

Figure 3.3 OASDI income rates and cost rates (from Trustees
of OASDI Trust Funds 1991, chart E)

also to be awakening to the long-term underfunding of OASDI
and considering changes in the program.

Under intermediate assumptions, annual OASDI shortfalls
in the mid-twenty-first century (that is, between 2041 and
2065) could be met with additional payroll taxes of about 1.9%,
beginning in 2040, for employer and employee each.[21] This solution would only make it more difficult to find funds to finance health and long-term care. It is possible, however, to
avoid some of the need for new revenues by (further) increasing
the age of retirement at full benefits under Old Age and Survivors Insurance (OASI); the current OASDI projections already
reflect the fact that this age was recently increased by law to
67, to be fully effective by 2022.

Whereas OASDI payroll tax increases would make Medicare financing more difficult, further increases in Social Security's normal retirement age could make it easier to finance the
health care of the aged by reducing the size of the population in
need of policy intervention. The age of Medicare eligibility has
not been prospectively increased, as OASI's has, but since 1982
Medicare benefits have been secondary to benefits provided by
employment-based insurance. Thus, inducing workers to re-

main employed beyond age 65 would shift some of the burden of health-care financing to their employment-based health insurance.

Recent studies of retirement behavior caution us, however, that a given increase in the Social Security retirement age would likely increase the age of actual retirement by fewer years for the average worker, in part because of the reluctance of those in poor health to delay retirement. Judging from the survey by Sammartino (1987), an increase in the Social Security retirement age from 65 to 70 would likely delay retirement by less than a year for the average worker. With average remaining life expectancy at age 65 already at about 17 years,[22] such a change would reduce Medicare's enrollee population by only a small fraction, and those eliminated would be among Medicare's healthiest enrollees. The potential for savings, as a percentage of total Medicare costs, would further decrease as the oldest old came to make up more and more of the Medicare population. So Social Security retirement age changes can reduce the retirement program's need for expanded payroll tax revenues, but we should not expect them to have much of a direct beneficial effect on Medicare's financing problems.

Cost Control through Prospective Payment

In 1983, HI initiated a radical change in the way it reimbursed hospitals, a change that has been very successful in reducing the growth rate of HI expenditures. Whereas HI had formerly based reimbursements on retrospective accounts of the cost of providing treatment, it began setting reimbursement prospectively by diagnosis, based on historical average treatment costs for patients within Diagnostic Rate Groups (DRGs). The goal was to make it most profitable for hospitals to provide services efficiently, and therefore at the lowest possible cost, while protecting the quality of service through expanded peer review. The SMI reimbursement system was unchanged: physicians retained the right to bill patients for more than SMI's allowable reimbursements. Hospitals also retained the right to bill Medicare retrospectively for costs of capital and medical education; this gave hospitals an incentive to substitute both physical and human capital for less-skilled labor (Sloan et al. 1988).

Medicare's adoption of its Prospective Payment System (PPS) was not an isolated event: efforts by other third-party payers to reduce hospital use were already reducing admissions and lengths of stay for younger patients by 1981 (Office of the Actuary, HCFA 1987). It is clear that PPS has similarly reduced the growth of HI expenditures; for the first sustained period in its history, HI's expenditures grew less rapidly between 1983 and 1990 than the taxable payroll that finances those expenditures.[23] Studies of the first few years of PPS (Guterman et al. 1988; Sloan et al. 1988; DesHarnais et al. 1987) revealed that rates of hospital admission and lengths of stay had decreased dramatically for HI patients. Labor costs per admission had also fallen, although reimbursible capital costs per admission had risen somewhat. Hospital cost savings had in fact been sufficient to allow sizable profits, despite the restrained growth in reimbursements.

A feared side effect of PPS was that providers would provide lower-quality care in the course of reducing cost, since reimbursements are set according to diagnosis and not to outcome. Hospital mortality rates did in fact rise for HI patients between 1984 and 1985, but this increase appears to be explainable by the PPS-induced change in inpatient case mix (Guterman et al 1988).

While decreased lengths of stay were an expected outcome of the change to prospective payment, reduced admissions were not. Some had feared, in fact, that PPS would lead to excessive admissions of patients with low needs for health care because such cases would be especially profitable for hospitals (Ellis and McGuire 1986). The decline in admissions which actually occurred may have been the result of expanded peer review and fear by hospitals of claims denials (Sloan et al. 1988), but both drops in admissions and length of stay also may have been due in large part to shifts of very long stay patients out of short-term hospitals and into rehabilitative, psychiatric, long-term or pediatric hospitals, all of which were exempted from PPS (Newhouse and Byrne 1988).

A shift toward provision of care in other settings was apparent. Hospital lengths of stay decreased the most for DRGs for which hospital subacute care is commonly needed, and for the oldest patients; at the same time, Medicare admissions to skilled nursing facilities were up (Guterman et al. 1988). And while hospital admissions fell, a shift toward outpatient treatment (also exempted from PPS) was apparent from the acceleration in outpatient reimbursements. Some of the savings of impatient hospital costs are clearly being spent on increased care in these other settings. While less formal settings may have lower resource requirements, allowing reductions in total costs, the full potential for savings under PPS will not be realized until all providers face equally strong incentives for cost control.

Long-Term Care: A Porous Safety Net

Family Support and Out-of-Pocket Financing

Medicare covers medical care as a matter of earned right, in the sense that every worker in covered employment for a sufficient length of time earns full HI coverage, regardless of need. SMI eligibility is likewise determined without regard to financial need. But long-term care in the United States is financed primarily by private funds and by public assistance: unlike social insurance, the availability of government aid is tied directly to ability to pay. In this second tier of the U.S. system, there is no earned right to skilled nursing care beyond HI's coverage of short recuperative stays. In fact, today's public assistance for those in nursing homes (through Medicaid) plays a role similar to that of the old age home of the early twentieth century, serving as a refuge of last resort for the frail and indigent elderly.

The most important source of private support is the family. Doty (1986) estimates that three-fourths of the functionally disabled elderly are helped solely by family members, compared to only about one-fifth who are cared for in nursing homes. The only public contribution, when care is provided directly by family members, is a federal income tax credit for dependent care expenses, available only to those who are employed and pay someone to care for their dependents. The credit cannot exceed 30% of expenses, with a maximum of $720 per dependent, and can be this large only for the lowest-income families.

When families are unable or unwilling to care for those who cannot care for themselves, more formal care becomes necessary. The recent growth in the oldest old population, the rising divorce rate, and the increasing rate of female labor force participation evidently strain the resources of families. Surveys indicate, however, that a peculiarly American desire for independence by the elderly and an unwillingness of some offspring to share living quarters, for emotional reasons, are among the most important barriers to family care (Doty 1986). There is evidence that financial necessity is an important factor promoting the maintenance of multigenerational extended-family households. Those with lower incomes are more likely to transfer resources to their elders within, rather than across, households, but are less likely to make transfers if public assistance payments are received by the elderly family members (Moon 1983).

Medicare and Medicaid Coverage

Medicare plays a very minor role in paying for long-term care; in 1986, for example, it financed only 1.6% of U.S. nursing home expenses, as table 2.1 shows. Official criteria distinguish institutions according to the complexity of the care they provide, categorizing them into Skilled Nursing Facilities (SNF), Intermediate Care Facilities (ICF), and institutions providing custodial care only. HI reimburses only for stays in SNFs and only for posthospital care of 100 days or less; the typical stay ends long before the limit is reached (Meiners 1983), in part because of the daily coinsurance rate of $81.50 applied after the first 20 days. Further, HI is structured in such a way that many nursing home administrators are unwilling to participate. HI's health, safety, and staffing standards are more rigorous than Medicaid's, and HI determines reimbursability after care has already been provided, subjecting the care provider to risk. As a result, many HI patients have been forced to spend "back-up" days as hospital patients, while looking for a nursing home in which to recuperate (Sorkin 1986). Home care reimbursable under HI is also limited to skilled care only, making providers wary of accepting any patients aside from those requiring sophisticated treatment.

Most private nursing care insurance has traditionally been designed to supplement these limited HI reimbursements, rather than to be the sole coverage for care which is unreimbursable under HI. For example, Medicare supplementary insurance, or "medigap" policies, usually meet HI copayments during short-term stays in skilled nursing facilities. As table 3.1 shows, HCFA's actuaries foresee a rapid increase in private health insurance reimbursements between now and the year 2000, replacing dwindling government funds. Nevertheless, private insurance accounted for less than 1.0% of nursing home expenditures in 1986, despite the fact that as many as 59% of the elderly may have owned an insurance policy with some coverage of long-term care (Meiners 1983).

Dwarfing Medicare and private insurance is Medicaid: in 1980, Medicaid paid almost half of all nursing home expenditures, although this figure had fallen to 41.4% by 1986. Medicaid was created in 1965 and is jointly operated and financed by the states and the federal government. Within broad federal guidelines, states have flexibility with regard to eligibility and coverage.

Medicaid's primary mission is to provide medical assistance for low-income persons who qualify for income-maintenance programs. Thus, parents and children who re-

TABLE 3.1
Distribution of Nursing Home Care
Expenditures by Source of Funds: 1980, 1986, and Projections for 2000 (%)

	1980	1986	2000
Direct patient payments	43.6	51.0	53.1
Private health insurance	0.9	0.8	4.8
Other private funds	0.6	0.7	0.8
Total private funds	45.1	52.5	58.7
Medicare	1.9	1.6	1.4
Medicaid	48.0	41.4	34.9
Other government funds	5.0	4.5	5.0
Total government funds	54.9	47.5	41.3

Source: Office of the Actuary, Health Care Financing Administration (1987), table 18.

ceive benefits from Aid to Families of Dependent Children are eligible for Medicaid assistance for a wide range of medical services. In fact, only 13% of Medicaid recipients was aged 65 or older in 1990; nevertheless, services provided to those aged 65 and older consumed 33% of Medicaid's budget.[24] There are two routes by which the elderly qualify for Medicaid assistance. First, every state must provide Medicaid to recipients of Supplemental Security Income (SSI), the federal-state program that is the primary source of public assistance to the elderly; SSI requires the demonstration of need relative to stringent limits on income and wealth. The second route is by qualifying for additional coverage which is optional for the states. A state may offer coverage (with federal matching funds) to all institutionalized individuals whose income and wealth are below specified limits, or to the "medically needy," defined as those whose income and wealth are low enough for eligibility after paying part of the out-of-pocket cost of current care.

An unfortunate result of this means-testing in Medicaid has been the impoverishment of healthy spouses of institutionalized recipients by the required "spending-down" of income and assets. This has been changed, as of 1989: noninstitutionalized spouses are now allowed to retain all of their own income and half of joint income, along with half of jointly held wealth up to $60,000. In addition, a "minimum monthly maintenance needs allowance," designed to provide a moderate income level, is now deducted from the institutionalized person's income before any required spend-down is computed. The reduced contribution to expenses required of spouses will insulate some from destitution; at the same time it will make Medicaid application more attractive to those who are not poor enough to quality for SSI, and is likely, therefore, to increase enrollment.

Regulations regarding prior transfers also have been relaxed recently. Until 1988, wealth transferred within the preceding two years had been counted against the SSI eligibility ceiling in order to guard against the achievement of eligibility through ostensible gifts to relatives or friends. But that "transfer penalty" has been eliminated, and in any case there was never any other means-testing with regard to relatives' ability to pay. Thus, Medicaid is an imperfectly targeted public assistance

program: those whose own resources barely exceed the specified limits are denied assistance, while others whose offspring
could well afford to help them have their care financed entirely
by Medicaid.

State Medicaid programs are required by federal law to pay
for skilled long-term nursing services for those who qualify for
the program, and many states also pay for nursing in intermediate care facilities and for emergency hospital services, prescription drugs, and eyeglasses. Some states provide prepayment for services through HMOs. State Medicaid programs
also have been required in the past to cover Medicare deductibles, coinsurance, and SMI premiums for those meeting Medicaid's eligibility requirements. Beginning in 1991, state Medicaid programs are required to provide this package to a greatly
expanded population of Medicare beneficiaries: those with incomes below the poverty level and wealth at or below twice the
SSI limit now qualify for this aid.

Medicaid's pricing system tends to produce a shortage of
available nursing home beds. Medicaid providers must accept
Medicaid's reimbursement as payment in full, at rates determined by states (except for hospital care, which is reimbursed
at Medicare rates). The supply of beds which is forthcoming
depends upon the state's reimbursement rate. Private patients
willing to pay higher rates tend to be served first, with the remaining available beds rationed among Medicaid patients,
their Medicaid-reimbursed demand exceeding supply (Scanlon
1980). In the 1970s and 1980s, this chronic shortage was wors-
ened by the efforts of many states to limit Medicaid costs by
rationing nursing home certificates-of-need.

The widespread and mistaken belief among Medigap enrollees that those supplementary policies, in combination with
Medicare, provide broad nursing home coverage (Rice 1987)
probably contributes to the scarcity of private long-term-care
insurance. But the existence and design of Medicaid may make
the purchase of additional private long-term-care insurance ir-
rational for many individuals (Pauly 1990). Since Medicaid is a
good substitute for private coverage, the latter may have had
little value for purchasers, aside from protecting assets set aside
for bequests from Medicaid's spend-down requirements. With
the recent liberalization of the transfer penalty, the most im-

portant remaining benefit to the individual of private long-term-care insurance may be the hope of prompter admission and higher-quality care than Medicaid could provide.

Financing and Prospective Payment

The federal government pays from 50% to about 80% of the cost of each state's Medicaid program, depending on a formula that uses the state's average per capita income to determine the federal share. Medicaid expenditures grew by about 11% per year between 1980 and 1990[25] and are projected to continue growing at about the same rate through 1995.[26] Expenditures on the elderly have grown nearly as rapidly, although the number of aged Medicaid recipients has actually declined since the mid-1970s.[27] Medicaid's $22 billion of 1990 expenditures on those aged 65 and over is about one-fifth of the amount spent by Medicare (HI and SMI) in the same year.[28]

In response to Medicaid's rising cost per aged recipient, a majority of states have adopted some form of prospective reimbursement. As with medical insurance, prospective reimbursement for nursing care aims to give providers greater incentive to provide services efficiently, at minimum cost, than they have under retrospective cost-based reimbursement. Frech (1985) has found nursing home operating expenses to be 41% lower in states providing simple flat rate reimbursements than in those states that reimbursed at cost, and generally similar cost savings in states with more complicated prospective payment systems. Several studies (Buchanan 1983; Harrington and Swan 1984) show prospective payment states to have had slower growth in average daily reimbursements per patient than retrospective payment states. These studies also indicate more patient days and certified beds with prospective reimbursement, indicating that savings may have enabled prospective payment states to ration care less stringently than other states. Prospective reimbursement requires further refinement, however, as it has been largely based on a two-tier dichotomy (skilled versus intermediate care). Nursing homes have had little incentive to admit the heavier-use patients within each reimbursement category. A number of experiments with more precisely targeted reimbursement have been undertaken more recently, such as New York State's system of Resource Utilization Groupings (RUGS).

Like HI's DRG system, RUGS divide patients by clinical characteristics into categories of homogeneous resource use.

Medicaid's Institutional Bias

While many state Medicaid programs extend coverage beyond skilled care to "intermediate" care, those needing only custodial care remain excluded from Medicaid. In addition, most states still require Medicaid home care to be "skilled." The resulting bias toward institutionalization is reinforced by Medicaid's eligibility limits, which are in practice more restrictive for home care than for institutional care. It is more difficult to spend one's income down to the eligibility ceiling when paying for less expensive home care than when institutionalized. And there is little government help for home-care patients in coordinating the delivery of physician, nursing, personal care, and transportation services (Brecher and Knickman 1985).

A shift from institutional to community-based care has promise for reducing Medicaid costs. Such a shift can be a practical impossibility in many an individual case, however, because it is difficult, once admitted to a nursing home, for a patient to reestablish an independent residence. In order to avoid the irreversible admission of patients who could be well served by a less intensive level of care, the States of Virginia and Massachusetts have conducted preadmission screening programs; these indicate that about one-sixth of nursing home admissions can be avoided without significantly reducing available care, provided that community-based alternative services are available to meet the needs of those denied admission (Hughes 1986).

Federal legislation enacted in 1981 permits states experimentally to waive Medicaid rules, providing home and community-based care for those who would otherwise be institutionalized, and most states have been granted waivers. In one experimental population, long-term home care was found to reduce institutionalization without increasing mortality or acute hospital use, but at increased total cost relative to a control group (Hughes et al. 1984). In states that have looser eligibility standards for nursing home patients than for other Medicaid recipients, a desire for equity creates pressure to expand the

Medicaid population, further contributing to increased cost, even while reducing cost in individual cases through deinstitutionalization. The aggregate experience of the states between 1983 and 1989 was a 70% increase in the number of recipients of Medicaid home health services without a decrease in the number of recipients in either skilled or intermediate care facilities.[29]

Summary

Most medical care for the aged, and much of the nursing care provided to the aged, are paid for through transfers from younger workers, either within families, through payroll taxes, or through other taxes which go into general revenues. Best-guess expectations of economic and demographic growth over the first half of the twenty-first century indicate that although it may be possible to prevent a decline in real transfers per recipient, it would be increasingly burdensome for workers to provide transfers whose value, per recipient, keeps pace with wages. Without changes in the way that we finance the medical and long-term care that Americans receive, their quantity and quality will probably fail to keep up with improvements in other aspects of the American standard of living.

Yet there are already serious gaps in coverage by public programs. These are primarily at the high end of the distribution of individual expenditures. Medicare hospitalization coverage ceases after 150 days; there is no ceiling on patient copayments for physician services; and Medicaid helps pay for long-term nursing care only for those patients whose expenses have left them destitute. If future transfers prove to be barely adequate to maintain care at its current level, then there will be little surplus with which to easily fill these gaps.

The best hope for improvements in quality of care and coverage is expanded self-financing. The especially large Baby Boom generation could augment future transfers by expanding current saving and earmarking it for the purpose of financing future health and long-term care. Since the largest gaps in coverage by public programs are for catastrophically large expenses incurred by an unfortunate minority, funded insurance is the logical vehicle for translating those current savings into future health and long-term care. Medicare's ill-fated catastrophic coverage would have been such a vehicle, financed by participant premiums, but its repeal brought to an abortive end this well-intended experiment in funded public insurance. Its absence leaves private insurance as the primary vehicle for expanded prefunding of health and long-term care.

The problems and promise of private insurance are explored in Chapter 4.

4

Problems of Private Insurance

AS THE AGE GROUP facing the greatest risk of catastrophic medical and nursing expenses and subject to the most certain limits to income growth, the retired elderly have the most to gain from insurance. Yet only a fraction of the retired population had health insurance before the federal government assumed the role of insurer by creating Medicare in 1965. Even today, the overwhelming majority has no private insurance covering long-term nursing care: a market for long-term-care insurance has emerged in the last five years, but the policies that it offers are expensive, and few own them. While those without long-term-care insurance can look to Medicaid for financial assistance, it is such an unattractive alternative that its availability is not by itself enough to explain the thinness of long-term-care coverage. Not only does Medicaid require very low levels of income and wealth of its recipients, it also makes its beneficiaries second-class nursing home customers by placing a below-market ceiling on the daily reimbursement rates that it will pay.

The market which is more fully developed is the market for Medicare supplements, or "medigap" policies. These most commonly fill the gaps that Medicare leaves for those who experience minor to moderately serious health problems, covering SMI's 20% coinsurance for physician care and HI's first-day deductible and its coinsurance for days 61–150 of hospitalization. Coverage for longer hospital stays is less common, and about one out of four elderly citizens has no Medicare supplement. Disproportionate among the uninsured are nonwhites, and those with lower incomes, less education, and poorer health (Rice and McCall 1985).

Why has the private insurance market been unable to provide the elderly with more complete insurance, especially for long-term nursing and catastrophic medical expenses? This chapter is devoted to market failure explanations for the limited coverage offered by private insurers, and to efforts by insurers to prevent market failure.

Adverse Selection

Reduced Coverage for Low-Risk Consumers

Insurance has value to those who consider themselves good risks, just as it does to those who see themselves as bad risks: a given loss causes equal hardship to members of either group. The essential difference between good and bad risks is in the premium they will be willing to pay to insure against a given loss: the customer with a lower probability of loss will not be willing to pay as high a premium as others, because a lower risk means a lower likelihood that the coverage will prove to be of value.

It is costly to collect detailed information about the riskiness of individual customers, however, so that it is not generally feasible for insurers to perfectly distinguish high from low risks; instead, lower risks are often placed into broad risk classes with higher risks and offered the same premium. What can then result, if customers are aware of their own individual odds, is adverse selection: the lower risks, for whom the insurance is a bad buy, are the most likely to decline coverage. In order to avoid losses, the insurer must then increase premiums to cover the losses of the remaining higher-risk population. It is possible for this process to continue until only the highest risks remain, paying actuarially fair but extremely high premiums. The danger of adverse selection is greatest where losses are most easily predictable by the consumer. In the case of health insurance, for example, this could include coverage for regular outpatient visits, or for drug treatments needed for a chronic illness.

In order to limit self-selection by high-risk customers, insurance companies build standard protections into their policies. In the case of health insurance, treatments for existing conditions are widely excluded, and enrollment generally is allowed only during limited open periods. But the most important defense against adverse selection is group coverage. Any large group which has been brought together for a purpose unrelated to risk of loss is unlikely to exhibit adverse selection as long as the group agrees to be covered in its entirety. Not only will the group's losses be approximately equal to population averages; a single group contract also provides marketing and administrative economies, so that insurers can offer group coverage at much lower rates than individual coverage. Thus, it is far more attractive for a low-risk individual to participate in group insurance than to be pooled with the generally poorer risks who would be willing to purchase individual policies.

The work force at a large establishment is a natural unit for group insurance. Insurance is not the reason for the group's formation, and current employment demonstrates that the group's health is probably at least as good as the health of the general population. In addition, contributions are a tax-deductible business expense, which reduces the effective price of insurance relative to other employee compensation. For these reasons, the vast majority (86% in 1988) of Americans under 65 who have private health insurance obtain it through the employment of a family member.[1] The retired, the unemployed, and uncovered employees of small establishments usually find comprehensive private coverage impossible to obtain at comparable rates.

Government can take up where employer-provided insurance leaves off, pooling the risks of nonworking families to make sure that insurance is available to high and low risks alike. Currently the federal government pools health-care risks in this way for the aged and disabled, but not the risk of long-term care. A few states have also experimented with health-care coverage for uncovered workers and their families. Whether government should participate more actively in insurance markets thinned by adverse selection, either as a regulator or as an insurer of last resort, is an important policy question. The next section is devoted to presenting an analytical framework within which to address that question. (It is more technical than the remainder of this volume and may be skipped by the reader who is not interested in theoretical underpinnings.)

A Model of Adverse Selection in Insurance Markets. Figure 4.1
is an "indifference curve" diagram, a standard tool used by
economists to visualize the opportunities available to consumers and to explain the choices that consumers make. Following
the seminal work of Rothschild and Stiglitz (1976), we adapt it
to the analysis of insurance decisions. In this case, insurance
enables consumers to choose combinations of wealth if in good
health (w_1), measured on the horizontal axis, and wealth if ill
(w_2), measured on the vertical axis. We take the consumer's situation without insurance to be the point E, where wealth
would be much greater in good health than in ill health. By purchasing insurance, the consumer can make wealth more equal
in the two possible states of the world, good health or illness.
This trade-off is shown as a movement along "budget lines"
like EH or EL; the less expensive the insurance coverage, the
steeper (and more attractive) the set of opportunities available
to the consumer. Lines EH and EL are budget lines for otherwise identical high- and low-risk consumers, respectively,
when insurance is fairly priced for each risk class. The lower
price offered to the low-risk consumer accounts for the steeper
slope of EL, providing the more attractive possible wealth outcomes.

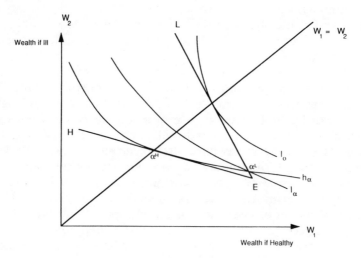

**Figure 4.1 Separating equilibrium for high- (H) and low- (L)
risk insurance customers**

Consumer choices depend on preferences, given market opportunities. The curved lines in figure 4.1, called indifference curves, represent these preferences graphically. The consumer is indifferent between any two points on a single curve but prefers to be on curves that are farther upward and to the right, since movement in that direction guarantees higher wealth, whether good health or illness is the ultimate outcome.

The consumers in figure 4.1 are "risk-averse," meaning that they prefer predictable wealth to unpredictable wealth. Risk is present when a consumer departs from the 45-degree line, which is a line of equal wealth in all states of the world, and risk aversion is the reason for the convexity of their indifference curves. They have an increasing reluctance to bear additional risk as they move away from the 45-degree line, requiring ever-larger additional increases in w_1 to maintain indifference as w_2 falls. And because of risk-aversion, if consumers are offered actuarially fair insurance, as they are in figure 4.1, their most preferred choice is "full insurance," where wealth is guaranteed to be equal in good health or bad. For high-risk consumers, choosing full insurance enables them to reach their highest attainable indifference curve h_α, at point α^H. The horizontal distance between E and α^H is the required premium, the amount by which a healthy person's wealth is reduced by insurance.

Adverse selection arises when insurers cannot readily distinguish high-risk customers, and happens as follows. The set of lower-premium contracts which would be fair for low risks is shown as line EL. Like high risks, low risks would prefer to have full insurance: for low risks, this would be the point where EL intersects the 45-degree line. But if such a contract appears in the market, high risks will also want to purchase it, because it dominates α^H, in good health or bad. In fact, if insurers cannot distinguish low risks from high, they must expect that any contract situated above and to the right of indifference curve h_α will be purchased by high risks, at a loss to the insurer. This limits the contracts which can be designed for and marketed to low risks. The most coverage obtainable by low risks at a rate that is fair for them is that depicted by the point α^L. Competition forces insurers to respond to consumer preferences, and the best that insurers can do in this regard without suffering losses is to offer the pair of contracts α^L and α^H. Rothschild and Stiglitz call this a "separating equilibrium," because low and high risks separate themselves by buying different policies, and because individual insurers could not increase profit by changing their policy offerings. In a separating equilibrium, low risks limit themselves to coverage which is just incomplete enough to be unattractive to high risks.

Actually, the situation depicted in figure 4.1 is only one possible competitive equilibrium, the one that obtains if high risks greatly outnumber low risks. But medical and long-term-care spending is typically highly concentrated among a small fraction of the population. In such markets, if there are sufficiently many low risk consumers, then there are contracts that can improve the situations of both high and low risks. With sufficiently many low risks to share the cost of a subsidy, it is worthwhile for them to help high risks obtain coverage on better terms; this is because the more satisfied high risks are with the insurance they obtain, the more coverage low risks can buy without high risks switching to their policies and driving up premiums (Miyazaki 1977; Spence 1978). [2] Thus, in figure 4.2, high-risks purchase contract β^H, whose price is less than actuarially fair, with the help of subsidies from low risks. The boundary for contracts which can be offered to low risks is thereby shifted to a higher indifference curve, h_β. Not all of the contracts on this boundary generate the required total subsidy from low- to high risks, however. The actuarially fair contract at its intersection with EL, for example, can provide no subsidy at all. One contract (β^L) on the boundary, however, if bought by low risks, includes just enough of a premium surcharge to cover the subsidy to high risks, enabling competitive insurers to break even. Thus, insurers could offer contracts β^H and β^L without suffering losses, and all consumers would consider their situations improved, relative to contracts with no subsidies. [3]

The subsidy per high-risk consumer in policy β^H was arbitrarily chosen and could have been either larger or smaller: consider, for example, a subsidy so great that high and low risks would pay the same premium. In this limiting case low risks would want full insurance, since there would be nothing to lose from high risks buying the same policies, so that both risk classes would obtain full insurance, indicated as γ in figure 4.2. At γ, all risks, high and low, are simply pooled. At the other end

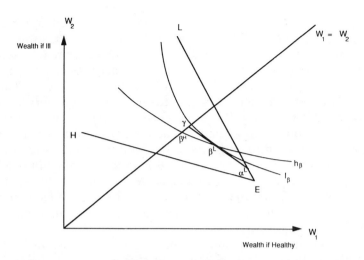

Figure 4.2 Subsidy equilibrium for high- (H) and low- (L) risk insurance customers

of the spectrum, contract α^L includes no subsidy at all. Thus, if we began with the largest possible subsidy and gradually decreased it to zero, the most attractive contracts that could be offered to low-risk consumers would trace out a locus $\gamma\alpha^L$.

This locus represents the upper boundary of contracts that can be offered to low-risk consumers without insurers suffering losses. Of these contracts, the one most preferred by low risks (just touching the highest reachable indifference curve l_β) is labeled β^L. In this case, the range of contracts meeting the economists' "Pareto criterion" for social choice (that there must be no other feasible combination that is better for some without being worse for others) is the locus $\gamma\beta^L$. Between γ and β^L, reductions in subsidies worsen the lot of high risks (reducing both w_1 and w_2 for them) while improving the situation of low risks (moving them toward their most preferred contract β^L), but further reductions in low-risk coverage beyond β^L move members of both risk classes to lower indifference curves. In this sense, β^L sets a floor below which coverage should not be allowed to fall.

The key question is whether the private market will provide cross-subsidizing insurance contracts on its own which include at least this much coverage, and the answer depends on the anticipated reactions of individual insurers to market entrants (Cave 1985). First, consider the polar-case assumption that firms always stop offering policies immediately whenever their profits turn negative and that this fact is well-known by all potential market entrants. Then the pair of policies β^H and β^L (with every insurer offering both) is a stable equilibrium for a competitive market. To lure low-risk customers away with a more generous policy than β^L (at a premium closer to fair) would leave incumbent firms selling only the underpriced and therefore unprofitable policy β^H. But then incumbents would cease offering β^H, and high risks as well as low would buy the new insurance, making it unprofitable. The knowledge that no entrant could succeed would prevent their entry, making (β^H, β^L) a stable equilibrium.

A change in the assumed behavior of firms leads instead to market failure. Before considering that alternative behavior, however, it is instructive to look more closely at the market equilibrium that occurs under our current behavioral assumption. In figure 4.2, the shifted set of feasible insurance offerings illustrates the distortion caused by an insurer's inability to distinguish between good and bad risks: the set of possibilities available to low-risk consumers has shifted from EL to the less attractive set $E_\alpha{}^L\gamma$. An external cost is thus imposed upon low risks: the more coverage they obtain, the more they must subsidize high risks in order to maintain separation in the market. This externality increases the price of coverage, for low risks, relative to fair insurance, and induces them to choose less than full coverage.

The property that low-risk consumers always obtain lower coverage than high-risk consumers, in a competitive equilibrium, generalizes readily from two to any larger number of risk classes. Only the class containing the highest risks ever obtains full insurance, and each class is always indifferent between its coverage and that obtained by the next less risky class, so that one's rate of loss replacement always declines with the riskiness of one's class (Cooper 1984; Cresta and Laffont 1987). Even if the insurance is sold by a monopolist, the pattern of declining coverage remains: in order to maximize profits, the monopolist increases premiums until the lowest-risk consumers are on the verge of buying no coverage at all, but sets premiums in such a way as to maintain the same separation that obtains in a competitive market (Stiglitz 1977).

None of this explains how adverse selection could cause a market to be thin, in the sense of many consumers having no coverage at all (as is the case with nursing care insurance, for example), despite aversion to risk. Market failure can occur, however, if we change our behavioral assumption such that potential market entrants expect incumbents to continue, for a time, to sell policies that become unprofitable.

This could occur, for example, if firms were slow to recognize the loss of profitability, a reasonable assumption in a model in which the firm's ability to collect information about consumers is already taken to be imperfect. In this case, incumbents would be vulnerable to new market entrants offering more attractive policies to low-risk customers. As long as older firms continued to offer β^H, new entrants could profitably lure away low risks by offering them less coverage at closer-to-fair premiums (in fact, any policy in the triangle bounded by EL, h_β, and l_β). But, eventually, the loss of low-risk customers would force incumbent firms to reduce the subsidy to high risks, causing high risks to switch to the new entrants' policies, making them unprofitable. Once those policies were withdrawn from the market, new entrants could earn profits by offering pairs of policies with lower coverage, and then the cycle would begin again. In short, the market would be unstable and unattractive to insurers.

Implications of the Model of Adverse Selection

The preceding section has shown that, when insurers cannot readily distinguish low risks from high, the coverage that can be offered without losses to low-risk consumers is limited to a rate of loss replacement so low that high-risk consumers find it unattractive. This is necessary, if low risks are to be offered correspondingly low premiums. Also, if low-risk consumers are sufficiently numerous, they can indirectly improve their own coverage by subsidizing the high-replacement-rate coverage bought by higher-risk consumers. As the price of this high-risk coverage falls, the rate of loss replacement for low risks can improve somewhat without high-risk consumers electing to buy the low-risk coverage. An equilibrium set of policies, one for each risk class, emerges if the insurance market is perfectly competitive and if the competitors expect any unprofitable offerings to be quickly withdrawn from the market.

But adverse selection would lead to market instability if insurers did not or were not allowed to quickly eliminate unprofitable policies. New market entrants could earn short-lived profits by offering low-risk consumers lower-priced, low-coverage policies requiring no cross-subsidizing premium surcharge. A market cycle would result: the loss of low-risk customers by established insurers would make it necessary to set higher prices for policies marketed to high risks, which in turn would make high risks more likely to switch to the new low-replacement-rate policies marketed to low risks, forcing the sellers of those policies to pare coverage even further. Ultimately, the evolving set of available policies would become less attractive to both risk classes than the initial set, from which low risks obtained greater coverage and high risks received a price subsidy; it would then be profitable to reintroduce cross-subsidizing coverage. In short, there would be no market equilibrium: no matter what policies were currently being offered, their profitability would be threatened by other, temporarily more profitable offerings. In such a market, the risk faced by any insurer would be great.

This model of market failure provides an explanation for thin insurance markets and a rationale for government intervention in the form of mandatory private or government-administered insurance. As long as there is inertia in the response of firms to changes in profitability, the insurance industry may be unable to reliably provide consumers with the socially optimal coverage. Under these circumstances, government intervention can improve the situation: government can stabilize the market by mandating coverage consistent with a social optimum and requiring consumers to buy the insurance.

There is really a continuum of Pareto-optimal coverage combinations (that is, those that are best in the sense that it is impossible to simultaneously improve the situations of both high- and low-risk consumers) from which policymakers could choose. The simplest such plan would be to require everyone to buy the same "pooled" policy (γ in fig. 4.2) from government or from a private insurer. This approach would entail the largest subsidy from low risks to high. At the other end of the spectrum would be a pair of policies requiring less cross-subsidization, more preferred by low risks because their coverage would be lower priced but less preferred by high risks because their coverage would be higher priced (that is, the combination β^H and β^L in figure 4.2).[4] Society's choice from among this set would depend primarily on its attitude toward redistribution among risk classes, since one class's loss is the other's gain, no pair of policies being unambiguously preferred by both classes. Pooled coverage does have a practical advantage over the other Pareto-optimal choices, however: it imposes the fewest informational requirements, requiring only an estimate of the average expected loss. In contrast, either a priori knowledge of preferences (that is, the locations of the indifference curves, which are revealed only by consumer choices) or a trial-and-error process are necessary in order to determine the limits of coverage that can be offered to low risks without making it equally attractive to high-risk consumers.

The surest way to avoid adverse selection in heath-care or long-term-care insurance is to make insurance available to young consumers, before the emergence of most chronic health problems (Pauly 1985). The earlier the insurance is sold, the less individuals can know about their ultimate risk of illness and disability, so that less adverse selection can occur. Or expressed another way, when consumers are young, they can insure not only against risks that have already made themselves evident but also against being judged bad risks by insurers later in life. Lengthening the terms of insurance contracts, however, trades one information problem for another: insurers and consumers must then contract for services to be delivered as much as six decades after the payment of initial premiums. Over such a long span, a few percentage points of unexpected inflation can accumulate into very much higher costs. Consider, for example, a provider of service benefits (that is, an insurer contracting to pay reasonable and customary charges) expecting 4% annual price inflation. If the actual inflation rate turned out to be a modestly higher 6%, then actual annual reimbursements would be more than double the expected amounts by the thirty-seventh year and triple by the fifty-eighth year.

Government could simply assume this inflation risk by underwriting a lifelong contributory plan. Alternatively, government or private insurers could reduce inflation risk by providing indemnity benefits (benefits paying a predetermined, fixed amount for each insured event) with optional inflation protection rather than service benefits; with indemnity benefits the risk of unexpected inflation is shifted entirely onto the purchaser. The optional annual inflation adjustment, such as many insurers provide as an option with life and disability insurance, would be available for an additional premium. The additional premium would be no less appropriate with government as the insurer, to compensate taxpayers for risk, than it is when the insurance is sold privately. Private insurers could offer inflation protection more cheaply by a preagreed adjustment than through periodic recontracting for higher coverage, because predetermined adjustments are less vulnerable to self-selection by those with developing health problems.

Another market of special importance for the elderly is also susceptible to adverse selection: the market for annuities. Annuities insure against outliving one's savings by guaranteeing a steady income as long as one lives. But to the extent that consumers have private information to use in figuring their life expectancies, this market, too, tends to dry up for all but those with relatively high risks: in this case, those who expect long life. Facing unfairly high annuity prices, consumers with shorter life expectancies are forced to accumulate other assets, in excess of amounts needed for their intended bequests, in order to provide themselves with income security. Fair annuities, if available, would provide a higher rate of return by enabling them to consume all of their assets during their lifetimes; individual savers with uncertain lifetimes cannot do this for themselves without risking the premature exhaustion of those assets.[5]

A familiar image of the harm done by the thin annuities market is that of a person with considerable wealth, in the form of the family home, whose standard of living has nevertheless fallen at retirement with the drop in money income. Unable to annuitize real estate wealth, and unable to obtain affordable rental housing, low-income retired persons may keep most of their wealth tied up in their homes, ultimately leaving those homes as bequests to their children, even when they are poorer than those children. Reverse Annuity Mortgages (RAMs), which enable an owner to sell a house in return for an annuity and then pay back a portion of that annuity to rent the house back, is one method for converting home equity into annuitized housing services; another is the Continuing Care Retirement Community (CCRC), which provides guaranteed lifetime residential and nursing service in return for a lump-sum entrance fee and subsequent periodic fees. The markets for both contracts, however, are limited by the same adverse selection that afflicts the market for ordinary annuities. For this reason, the approach that has the greatest promise for helping families make full use of their wealth is the promotion of early commitments to RAMs, CCRCs, and other annuitized residential arrangements, entered into at a stage of life when health and longevity risks are not yet well-known to consumers. Both RAMs and CCRCs are discussed at greater length in Chapter 5.

Scale Economies

Finally, the thinning effects of adverse selection and of inflation risk on insurance markets are magnified by the administrative scale economies that characterize the industry. When enrollment for any kind of insurance is low, premiums must reflect a high administrative cost per enrollee. This is especially so when the policy is in force over a long period, during which policyholders disperse geographically. Insurers may wish, for example, to make nursing coverage contingent upon preadmission screening, a process that is administratively cumbersome if enrollees migrate widely in retirement.

By mandating coverage under a single plan, government could centralize information, take full advantage of other scale economies, and eliminate the need for competitive marketing, making premiums more affordable. A widely cited long-term-care insurance prototype (Meiners 1983) included premiums for individual coverage that exceeded losses by 40% and by 25% for group coverage; these are the federally recommended maximum loadings for Medicare supplements. In contrast, Medicare (HI and SMI combined) had 1990 administrative expenses that were only 2.1% of benefits paid, thanks to its massive scale, its absence of marketing costs, and the assumption of inflation risk by taxpayers. Social Security Disability Insurance, which imposes a considerable burden of eligibility determination upon government, had administrative costs that were

only 2.8% of benefits in the same year.[6] With such low administrative costs, a public insurance program could impose an additional premium to compensate future taxpayers for inflation
risk and still offer consumers a much better buy than private
coverage. The cost advantage of mandatory coverage, achieved
through scale economics and the avoidance of adverse selection, is a strong argument in its favor.

Evidence of Adverse Selection

Empirical evidence of adverse selection by elderly health
insurance customers is scarce, because 99% of those eligible
for Medicare elect full coverage at rates that are heavily subsidized by taxpayers. And the majority of Medicare enrollees who
supplement their coverage with private medigap plans may be
so poorly informed about the gaps they are filling and the coverage they are purchasing that their selections have little to do
with actual risk. For example, most enrollees believe that Medicare and medigap plans provide broad nursing home coverage,
even though almost all elderly nursing home entrants must
turn elsewhere for funds (Rice 1987). Medigap plans typically
supplement only those limited nursing services that first qualify for Medicare, namely, short-term recoveries from acute illness. Nevertheless, Wolfe and Goddeeris (1991) have found, in
a sample of recently retired Medicare enrollees, that those with
higher recent health-care expenditures are more likely to purchase medigap insurance and to have high current expenditures.

There is also indirect evidence from the Rand Health Insurance Experiment (discussed below) that optional supplemental
coverage for younger families is subject to adverse selection
(Marquis and Phelps 1987). As part of the experiment, families
were offered hypothetical supplements to their current insurance and also asked about their expected future health-care expenditures. Those who reported higher expected future expenditures were also more likely to say they would purchase the
hypothetical supplement and were, in fact, more likely to have
higher subsequent medical costs. In both studies, the relationship between high expenditures and insurance remained after
controlling for family demographic characteristics, making it
impossible for insurers to eliminate adverse selection by using
those family characteristics to set premiums.

Adverse selection has also been detected empirically in the market for private annuities: those who buy them tend to be high risks, living longer than average. Warshawsky (1988) estimates that this adds about 10–15 cents to the cost of each dollar's worth of annuity coverage compared to fair pricing. The benefit to the average citizen of a mandatory public annuity like Social Security is therefore substantial, especially when the savings in marketing and administrative costs are also taken into account.

There is also a growing body of evidence concerning self-selection in the decision by working-age families whether or not to join a Health Maintenance Organization (HMO). While traditional fee-for-service (FFS) plans usually minimize the coverage choices offered to the customer, in order to avoid adverse selection, many employers offer HMO membership as an alternative to FFS coverage; in fact, federal law permits HMOs to offer substitute coverage, at the individual worker's option, to workers at any firm that employs at least 25 and offers traditional coverage.

Surprisingly, there is much recent evidence that the self-selection that occurs in the HMO versus FFS decision is favorable to HMOs, on balance, rather than adverse. HMO members tend to be younger and to have less chronic illness (Dowd and Feldman 1985), and prior to HMO enrollment they also tend to have used fewer medical services and to have incurred lower medical costs than their traditionally insured peers (Jackson-Beeck and Kleinman 1985). The elderly who elect HMO membership as an alternative to standard Medicare coverage also have been found to have lower preenrollment utilization (Eggers 1980; Eggers and Prihoda 1982).

This finding is significant because HMOs consistently have been found to have lower costs per enrollee than traditional care providers. If HMOs spend less because, as both insurer and care provider, they have greater incentive than traditional providers to use medical resources efficiently, then the promotion of HMOs reduces overall health-care costs. But if the real difference is that people who require less expensive care elect HMOs over FFS coverage, permitting HMOs to skim off the low-cost patients and leave high-cost patients to traditional insurers, then HMO growth really leaves total costs unaffected. And, indeed, some of the apparent efficiency advantage of HMOs disappears when one controls for the better reported health of their members (Welch 1985a).

Since HMOs tend to provide broader coverage than traditional insurance, we would expect adverse, rather than favorable, selection. The finding that those who choose HMOs tend to be at less risk than those who choose traditional insurance suggests that high risks select traditional coverage for some other reason than differences in coverage, and a likely candidate is the cost of transition from one coverage to another. The chronically ill may be the least likely to switch into (or out of) HMOs because a change in coverage requires one to switch doctors. Thus, even though the coverage offered by HMOs may be attractive to the high- and low-risk alike, it is available at the lowest transition cost to those who are currently healthy.

Transition costs tend to counteract the effects of adverse selection because they discourage switches from one coverage to another. As closely as current risk and current coverage might be related if only it were costless for consumers to learn about and change insurance policies, actual transition costs introduce a dampening effect in which past history also influences current coverage. A family anticipating maternity care, for example, and choosing a plan that covers that care, might remain in the plan long after their special insurance needs have been met rather than incur the cost of another change. The result would be regression to the mean, in the years following a switch: the family's risk would fall in the direction of the population averages (Welch 1985b). For this reason, studies of self-selection which simply compare preenrollment utilization between switchers (to HMOs, for example) and nonswitchers probably overstate the long-run effects of self-selection. HMO enrollees may be especially unlikely to have chronic illnesses in the year of enrollment, but their likelihood of developing chronic illness can be expected to be closer to average in each subsequent year that they are enrolled.

Transition costs can even prevent convergence to equilibrium altogether, leading instead to a cycle (Neipp and Zeckhauser 1985). What can give rise to a cycle is the creation of new insurance pools, with younger workers taking the places of retiring workers in the labor force. Since switching into a new plan is most disruptive to those receiving the most care, the newest plans tend to have the youngest and healthiest populations. As the loss experiences of older plans deteriorate, it becomes necessary for them to increase their premiums and, therefore, increasingly difficult for them to enroll new members. Even new plans soon begin to experience this gradual increase in costs, and the oldest plans eventually reach the point where they are completely unable to enroll new members. The many insurance options offered to U.S. government employees under the Federal Employees Health Benefits Program appear to go through this life cycle (Price and Mays 1985).

We can draw the following conclusions concerning any expansion of health insurance for the elderly. If coverage were optional, its price would be increased by adverse selection. If consumers were provided with choices among competing private plans, a possible outcome would be a cycle in which the youngest would choose new, low-cost plans while the oldest would be covered by high-cost plans which could not compete for new customers. The alternative of a single mandatory insurance plan is attractive in that it would avoid adverse selection and thereby provide the average consumer with fairer and more stable insurance premiums.

Moral Hazard

Overutilization of Services

Moral hazard is the tendency of insurance itself to induce losses. Whereas adverse selection is a distortion in the demand for insurance, moral hazard is a distortion in the behavior of those who are already insured, reducing their aversion to losses. It is moral hazard that makes 100% coverage impractical and undesirable for most risks, despite the attractiveness of full insurance to risk-averse consumers.

Few losses are pure acts of God. In the case of an insurable medical event, virtually all patients exercise some choice over the care they receive: they may be free to choose where to be treated, in what class of hospital accommodation, by whom, and whether to follow the complete recommended course of treatment. To the extent that consumers have control over treatment and pay for it out-of-pocket, they will be concerned about the prices of goods and services recommended by health professionals: those who pay for eyeglasses out-of-pocket, for example, surely decide how many to buy and where to buy them as carefully as they would in shopping for any other good. But insurance, by bearing part of the cost, reduces the price of treatment to a consumer, and, as with other products, a lower price usually means a greater quantity demanded. Moral hazard, then, is really just an ordinary response of demand to price, but it imposes a regrettable trade-off in the design of insurance: the greater the protection that insurance provides against a particular loss, the more of that loss may occur.

The reader may wonder why greater demand for care is a problem, since more care may lead to better health. The sense in which moral hazard causes demand to be excessive is the following: insured consumers tend to demand additional care, as long as its benefit exceeds the consumer's portion of its cost, even if the benefit of that service is less than its true cost. Insurance can induce demand to be excessive in terms not only of quantity but also of quality, leading to "Cadillac care" for those with insurance (Frech and Ginsberg 1987). And not all of the increased demand is translated into increased care for consumers. By reducing the price to the consumer, insurance reduces the consumer's incentive to shop around, enabling providers to exercise a heightened degree of monopoly power in the pricing of their services.

The costs of extra spending due to moral hazard are not only a problem for insurers but also ultimately for the insured, since their premiums must ultimately cover the increased expenditures. Moral hazard increases the cost of insurance for any loss over which the insured can exercise control. In essence, the consumer's problem is that greater protection against losses can only be obtained at the cost of compromising one's own thriftiness as a health-care consumer and, even more important, the thriftiness of one's fellow insurance pool members.

Elective Care and Safeguards against Moral Hazard

There are necessities of life, such as staple foods, for which price increases barely diminish demand. Also included among these necessities are life-sustaining medical services. Victims of appendicitis, for example, demand exactly one appendectomy, no matter how high the price; furthermore, they would not buy a second appendectomy at any price. When demand is relatively unresponsive to price, we call it "price-inelastic." In contrast to necessary care, we expect more elective care to be more responsive to price, or "price-elastic." It is rational for an insurer to provide the most complete coverage for the services with the least price-elastic demand, because with these services there is the least extra demand created. This pattern of coverage also makes the most efficient use of a society's scarce medical resources (Ramsey 1927). In practice, insurers do in fact provide lower percentage reimbursements for more elective services (outpatient care, for example), requiring the patient to pay the remaining percentage as a copayment.

One traditional reimbursement strategy is to provide service benefits, reimbursing all claims for any qualifying ailment according to a single comprehensive schedule, which typically reimburses a fraction of total expenses above a deductible, up to a maximum out-of-pocket amount. The rationale for this scheme is that the smallest expenses, like those for office visits, are usually the easiest for consumers to control, whereas further losses may be unavoidable once an illness has become catastrophic. A national health plan proposed years ago by Martin Feldstein (1971) is an example of a plan that would have imposed the greatest copayments at the low end: families would have been subject to an annual deductible and then have paid a fraction of costs, up to an annual family maximum that would have been scaled to income. Thus, a family with a member fighting a prolonged battle with cancer would have been insured for most of the cost, but families without current catastrophic expenditures would have paid much of the cost of treatment for routine illnesses. Medicare's recently repealed catastrophic coverage would have had a similar design: HI would have limited each person's inpatient hospital costs to a single deductible, and SMI would have set a maximum annual payment to physicians.

Service benefits have been widely abandoned by insurers in recent years because of the blank check that they provide to patients and to providers as their agents. For example, a surgical procedure may be necessary to sustain life, but the length of the recuperative hospital stay may be largely a matter of comfort for the patient and a matter of indifference to the provider, if reimbursed at cost. In such a case, an "indemnity" payment, providing a predetermined maximum dollar amount toward the total treatment of the specific ailment, is one way to limit reimbursements to the amount necessary for treatment, without boosting demand for additional services.

The out-of-pocket price of care to the patient, and the resulting incentive to limit utilization, depend not only on the reimbursement schedules of public and private insurance but also on the way that they fit together. By bridging Medicare's gaps, medigap policies provide access to subsidized Medicare reimbursements, so that Medicare and the typical medigap policy, taken together, provide an umbrella of first-dollar coverage which virtually guarantees excessive demand for insurance and care. Medigap insurance covering HI and SMI deductibles and SMI's coinsurance is now so widely held that changes in Medicare copayments can do little to prevent the overutilization of medical resources without limitations on medigap coverage of those copayments.

Private coverage of nursing care has been limited by the difficulty of clearly distinguishing necessary care from medically unnecessary household services. Under many existing policies, nursing care is covered only if certified as necessary by a physician, and home care is often limited to skilled care. For less-skilled care, an insurer may require an objective assessment of the claimant's ability to function independently.

A related problem arises in connection with Medicaid's nursing home reimbursement policies. There is "market-basket" moral hazard (Paringer 1983) when a potential Medicaid recipient faces the decision whether or not to enter a nursing home, because Medicaid payments not only lower the price to the patient of nursing services but also lower the cost of most basic living needs such as food and shelter. This biases a patient's choice of setting toward institutionalization as opposed to arranging for home care. In addition, the choice of nursing home can be subject to moral hazard in a more familiar form: consumers have little incentive to choose low-priced over high-priced facilities, since the difference in price is covered by Medicaid rather than out-of-pocket.

Regulators in some states have made it difficult to limit nursing insurance coverage to the most necessary services. While the goal may have been to protect poorly informed consumers from exploitation, the effect has been to erect an additional barrier to the growth of private insurance (Meiners 1983). New York State, for example, has required that insurers offer to fill Medicare's deductible and coinsurance gaps before covering catastrophic nursing expenses, while Wisconsin has banned lifetime deductibles exceeding 60 days. Such regulations prevent consumers from carefully targeting their scarce premium dollars toward catastrophic nursing coverage, a much greater threat to financial security than the lower-end gaps in Medicare. Consumer protection would be better achieved through greater required disclosure by insurers and through public education.

Evidence of Moral Hazard

The expectation that more elective care should be more responsive to price is generally borne out in studies of health-care utilization by samples of individual consumers. In particular, outpatient visits to physicians are usually found to have more elastic demand than inpatient care (Pauly 1986; Feldstein 1988; Farley and Monheit 1985). Studies from microdata have estimated that the total demand for health care has a price elasticity in the range -0.2--0.5, implying that every 1.0% increase in out-of-pocket costs, from one insurance plan to another, decreases utilization of services by 0.2%–0.5%, on average. An extrapolation of these estimates suggests that a doubling of required coinsurance (a 100% increase) might cut health-care expenditures by about 20%–50%.

But adverse selection would impart an upward bias to moral hazard estimates produced with microdata: those expecting the greatest future expenditures tend also to have the most complete coverage and, therefore, to face the lowest price for health care. For this reason, the Rand Corporation conducted a large-scale health-insurance experiment, enrolling consumers into five plans which varied according to deductibles and coinsurance. As the adverse selection argument had led them to expect, the Rand researchers estimated an overall elasticity at the low end of the range of previous estimates, about −0.2 (Manning et al. 1987). They found, for example, an 18% difference in the cost of services used between those whose coinsurance rate was one-quarter and those who paid double that rate (that is, coinsurance of one-half). They also confirmed the earlier finding that outpatient services were more affected by insurance than were inpatient services. Surprisingly, however, they found no difference in price-elasticities between emergency and other services, or between well-care and other medical services.

To discourage excessive outpatient care by requiring substantial copayments would be short-sighted if poor coverage of outpatient visits were to result in more hospital admissions, at increased total cost (Roemer et al. 1975). The Rand experiment found, however, that outpatient visits and hospital admissions appear to be complements, not substitutes: those who were required to pay for a larger share of outpatient care used less inpatient care as well.

Less is known about the price-elasticity of demand of the elderly, as a subgroup, for health care. The near-universality of Medicare coverage in this age-group leaves little cross-sectional variation in the out-of-pocket price of care, and the Rand experiment excluded older consumers. There is, however, evidence that medigap insurance substantially increases both hospitalization and physician-care expenditures, increasing Medicare reimbursement for both kinds of care in the process (Taylor et al. 1988).[7] If this is the case, then the medigap premium buys more than just private coverage, it also effectively increases Medicare coverage. A tax on medigap premiums (possibly scaled according to the extent that individual policies subvert Medicare's low-end cost-sharing) would be an appropriate way to compensate Medicare for its unintended subsidy of medigap policies.

Regarding the demand for skilled nursing care, the evidence from a pair of studies indicates price-elasticities of −0.1– −0.2 (Chiswick 1976; Scanlon 1980). Demand for intermediate and custodial care is likely to be more elastic, because less skilled services tend to be more elective.

The question of the substitutability of services in inpatient and outpatient settings is at least as important in connection with nursing care as with medical care. It is often argued that the nursing home population is excessively large because of Medicaid's bias toward institutionalization, and that easier access to home nursing care could actually reduce costs. The danger in offering home health coverage is the "woodwork effect" (Leutz and Greenberg 1985), wherein noninstitutionalized subscribers may "come out of the woodwork" and initiate covered home care, swamping any savings from deinstitutionalization of other beneficiaries. The finding in most states that have liberalized medical coverage of home care has been that costs have increased: home services do not appear primarily to substitute for institutionalization but rather to meet the needs of a clientele that previously was not well served by Medicaid (Brecher and Knickman 1985).

Pay-as-You-Go Financing of Employer-Provided Insurance

Not all Medigap insurance is prefunded: of the 22 million elderly covered by private health insurance in 1988, 10 million were covered by employment-related policies,[8] and most employer health plans are funded on a pay-as-you-go basis, that is, financed out of current revenues. While ERISA (the Employee Retirement Income Security Act) imposes funding requirements for pension plans, there are no corresponding federal rules governing the funding of health-insurance obligations. The unfunded liabilities of employers threaten to leave a large segment of the private health insurance sector as vulnerable as public transfer programs to future increases in the retiree-to-worker ratio.

The extent of the future liabilities already accrued by U.S. firms who provide retiree health plans has recently been dramatized by discussions surrounding the possible reform of accounting standards; a draft set of standards incorporating reforms was proposed by the Financial Accounting Standards Board in 1989. These new standards would require employers to report accrued liabilities for postretirement benefits as expenses spread over an employee's entire period of service (with decrements for expected turnover and mortality). For any company expecting growth in postretirement benefits, the result of the new standards would be a reduction in reported profits. Estimates of liabilities already accrued by U.S. employers by the late 1980s for postretirement health benefits have been strikingly high, ranging from $170 billion to $446 billion, and the cost of annual accruals of future benefits, when accounted for as current expenses, has been estimated to be more than four times as great as current pay-as-you-go costs (Warshawsky 1989).

The proposed accounting standards would actually have no direct effect on the degree of funding of employer-provided plans. Their most important direct effect would be to reveal to investors and workers the true magnitudes of future benefit commitments. If, however, these standards are adopted and future liabilities come to be reflected in current-year expenses as if they were prefunded, then shifts from pay-as-you-go to prefunding should be easier for management to make, since reported profits would no longer be reduced by such a shift. Of course, the required reporting of accrued expenses, if adopted, is also likely to cause many employers to cut back on promised benefits, in order to increase their current reported profits.

For employers who choose to prefund their employees' postretirement health benefits, there are two tax-advantaged methods for doing so (Klein and Petertil 1986), but in each case the tax deductibility of employer contributions may be unreasonably constrained. Employers may contribute to a Voluntary Employees Beneficiary Association (VEBA), a vehicle for funding postretirement health and life insurance benefits, but the amount of contributions (plus interest) that the employer may deduct from taxable income is limited to a level amount, over the employee's working life, sufficient to pay future benefits under assumptions of a continuation of current claim experience and of no future inflation. Another possibility, for employers who provide defined-benefit pension plans, is to create a separate 401(h) account for the funding of postretirement health benefits. But employer contributions are limited to a maximum of 25% of current pension fund contributions, even if the scale of health-benefit obligations calls for greater relative contributions, and even if an overfunded pension plan requires no current contributions.

These limitations on employer contributions could be removed, making prefunding more attractive to employers, by making tax rules consistent with the proposed accounting standards. If benefit accruals are to be accounted for as a current expense, in such a way as to fully reflect expected inflation and changes in experience, then employers could also be allowed to deduct contributions in that same amount to a health benefits fund. This would give prefunded plans the same tax advantages that have been enjoyed by pay-as-you-go health plans, regardless of the employer's current contributions to defined-benefit pension plans, eliminating a bias in the tax law against prefunding.

Summary

Where insurance is unavailable to elderly consumers at actuarially fair premiums, adverse selection is the likely culprit. Where required coinsurance rates are high, especially for elective care, insurers are probably attempting to minimize the effects of moral hazard. And where private coverage provided by employers has been underfunded, much of the blame has been due to the invisibility of employers' accrued benefit obligations.

To the extent that adverse selection accounts for the thinness of the catastrophic medical and long-term-care insurance markets, government could attack the problem directly by introducing mandatory contributory coverage: the creation of a mandatory pool would prevent adverse selection among the retired just as it does for employment groups. Uniform premiums and coverage would require good risks to subsidize bad risks, but good risks may prefer this to the thin coverage available in the private market. Uniform coverage would be simple to administer, and it would avoid the cycles of good and then worsening experience that can occur when multiple offerings are made available. Efforts to expand decentralized private insurance offerings must confront the joint problem of adverse selection and inflation risk. Private insurers and consumers are unlikely to join in early insurance agreements, in advance of the emergence of differential risks, unless they are convinced that they are not subjecting themselves to unreasonable inflation risk by doing so. It may be in the public interest for government to become a participant in long-term-insurance contracts, for example, by allowing insurers to invest the proceeds from the sale of these policies in special government bonds with inflation-indexed interest rates, in order to stimulate the growth of the private market.

Coinsurance for low and moderate levels of expenditure, on the other hand, could be eliminated only at great peril to the insurer, especially in the case of outpatient care. If anything, the combination of Medicare and the typical medigap insurance policy now requires too little coinsurance of most elderly for low and moderate expenses. Increasing required copayments for those with medigap policies would improve this situation.

Where employer-provided health insurance is underfunded, as most of it is, one cause is a tax policy that inadvertently favors pay-as-you-go financing with a greater tax advantage. Coordination of tax policy with sensible reforms to accounting standards, namely, permitting deductibility of contributions up to the liability accruals which would be reported as current expenses, would remedy this imbalance between funded and unfunded benefits.

Changes initiated by government are not the only possible response to private insurance market shortcomings. The private sector itself has introduced a number of innovative insurance vehicles in recent years, designed to overcome the shortcomings of traditional offerings. Along with discussions of possible reforms to public programs, the next chapter includes descriptions of those innovations and assessments of the role that each could play in helping to adequately insure today's working generations during and after the upcoming demographic transition.

5

Financing Twenty-first Century Care: Alternative Approaches

Medical Care

Because the use of medical services rises less rapidly with age than the need for nursing care, the projected growth in demand for hospital and physician services as the population ages is likely to be less rapid than the growth in demand for long-term care. Still, as was shown in Chapter 3, Medicare's HI portion is projected to be underfunded, at current payroll tax rates, by the late 1990s, and SMI and Medicaid spending will be subject to the same upward forces as HI, namely, an aging population and the understandable desire of beneficiaries to take advantage of improvements in medical care. Even now, Medicare and private medigap insurance together provide generally inadequate coverage for catastrophically high hospital and physician expenses. The first part of this chapter discusses possible means of shoring up the system of medical insurance for the aged.

Finding New Revenues for Public Programs

Of the possible remedies for Medicare and Medicaid financing problems, the one that would alter the structure of these programs the least would be to supply them with increased tax revenues, either through higher rates for existing taxes or the introduction of new taxes. Earmarked payroll taxes, general revenues (which include income and excise taxes) and enrollee premiums currently pay for these programs. The first are paid primarily by the nonelderly, because of their greater labor earnings, the second by both young and old, and the third is paid only by the over-65 population. In the long run, the degree to which each of these taxes transfers income across generations,

93

from young to old, is of paramount importance and should be a guiding criterion in exploiting future sources of increased revenue.

In the short run, however, ability-to-pay considerations are more compelling. While the aged are arguably as affluent on average as other Americans, their incomes are more likely to be fixed (in real, if not nominal, terms) than those of younger workers, and their abilities to supplement their incomes through increased earnings are much more limited. A tax or premium to be borne after age 65 can be anticipated during working years and saved for only if enacted and well publicized with a decade or more of lead time. Even if this behavioral response is weak, advance notice of a tax or premium at least allows workers the opportunity to spread its burden over their working lives. For this reason, levies on aged beneficiaries become more defensible on ability-to-pay grounds, the longer the planning horizon. Most important, any resulting increase in saving by today's workers, in anticipation of future taxes or premiums, can promote capital investment and make it easier for future workers and wealth holders alike to meet the health-care demands of an aging population.

Among broad-based taxes which could be increased are personal income taxes, sales taxes (or their virtual equivalent, the "value-added tax" paid by producers and passed on to consumers), and excise taxes on alcohol and cigarettes (sometimes called "sin taxes"). Of these, all would be borne primarily by younger generations, so that none would reduce the extent of intergenerational transfers in health-care financing, but the first would be more progressive than the others. Alcohol and cigarette taxes are nevertheless attractive as a means of deterring unhealthy and ultimately expensive behavior, and of increasing the share of health-care costs borne by high users of care (Long and Smeeding 1984). And these excise taxes are at historically very low levels: because they are levied on a nominal per unit basis, inflation effectively reduced rates by 50%–75% between 1950 and 1990 (Congressional Budget Office 1990), when modest increases were enacted. Their major limitation as sources of earmarked funding for Medicare or other specific programs is their narrow base and the resulting potential instability of their revenues: purchases of cigarettes and alcohol could rapidly decline due to lifestyle changes and due to the tax increases themselves. This makes their consumption a much less reliable tax base than payroll, so that earmarked excise taxes on cigarettes and alcohol would make Medicare financing even more uncertain than it is today. For this reason, these taxes should continue to go into general revenue, even if their rates are increased.

Several approaches are available for increasing the share of costs borne by the older generation of program enrollees. The simplest would be to increase the SMI premium. In the early history of the program, premiums were set at levels sufficient to pay 50% of SMI's costs, whereas they cover only about one-quarter today.[1] Because Medicaid pays SMI premiums for its eligible population, a higher premium would have little effect on the poorest elderly. The additional revenue from a premium paying for half of SMI, however, would not by itself be enough to solve Medicare's financing problems. If such a premium were imposed today, it would increase Medicare's total revenues by only about one-eighth, a small increase compared to the magnitude of the shortfalls predicted for the early twentieth century.

Additional revenues also could be obtained through new taxes on Medicare eligibles, such as the income-tax surcharge that was to have been imposed as part of the Medicare Catastrophic Coverage Act. Revenues from such a surcharge could be earmarked for specific trust funds, just as income taxes on OASI benefits are now returned to the OASI Trust Fund. An income tax surcharge would have the advantage of administrative simplicity, since it would work through the existing income-reporting and tax-collection structure and could take advantage of the progressivity already embodied in personal income taxes. Income tax rates are in fact even more progressive for older taxpayers than for others, because the nontaxability of social security benefits for lower-income tax payers leaves many with no income-tax liability at all. A proportional surcharge on income taxes, such as would have been earmarked for catastrophic coverage, would be highly progressive in the same way, perhaps excessively so. But varying the mix of an income tax surcharge and a flat increase on SMI premiums could roughly achieve any desired degree of progressivity with respect to current taxable income.

The tax treatment of private pensions and OASI benefits suggests a second approach to taxing the incomes of beneficiaries. Since employer contributions to pensions are tax deductible for the employer, they are taxed as income at the time of receipt; this, too, is the rationale for taxing one-half of Social Security benefits. (In each case, employee contributions are out of income that is already subject to personal income tax.) By the same reasoning, both private insurance and Medicare coverage paid for by employers are like tax-free income when they become available, and they could be taxed as such. A tax on the value of coverage would be preferable to a tax on reimbursements, since the former would be borne by all who benefit from insurance, whereas the later would tax only the medically unfortunate. A tax on the insurance value of Medicare would be progressive: if a flat amount, representing the estimated value of insurance, were added to the taxable incomes of all who filed returns, actual increases in tax liability would vary according to marginal tax rates of taxpaying units. Taxing employer-provided coverage for retired workers would be an even more progressive revenue source, since those with coverage are also more likely than others to have private pension income.

The distorting effect of supplemental, or medigap, coverage on Medicare claims is an additional reason to consider a tax on private insurance. Long and Smeeding (1984) have proposed a surcharge on premiums paid for supplemental insurance; if revenues were earmarked for the Medicare trust funds, this surcharge would partly compensate Medicare for additional Medicare spending undertaken by those for whom employer-provided insurance fills in Medicare's gaps. In addition, a surcharge would actually dampen demand for medigap coverage, indirectly reducing Medicare spending.

Imposing this surcharge only on medigap premiums and not on employers who self-insure rather than pay premiums would exacerbate the current unequal treatment of those with and without employer-provided coverage, however. Fairness would dictate a similar surcharge on coverage provided by firms that self-insure.

An alternative to the surcharge would be for each medigap reimbursement to be made to bear more of the costs of the

Medicare coverage to which it provides access. For example, medigap policies which now pay SMI's 20% coinsurance could be required to actually cover a higher percentage of below-catastrophic costs, such as 30% of costs up to $5000, with SMI paying only the remainder. Insurers covering the SMI and HI deductibles could similarly be required to cover a dollar amount greater than the usual deductible, reducing Medicare's liability. Not only would this reduce Medicare's costs, it also would give medigap insurers greater incentive to limit their coverage to nonelective care, since they would have to pass on to consumers a greater portion of any insurance-induced costs. For those without supplementary insurance, Medicare copayments would be unaffected.

Prefunding of Public Programs

Payroll taxes or other taxes on workers could be tapped for new revenues without increasing the burden of intergenerational transfers if, instead of being used to finance current expenditures, the new revenues were accumulated in HI, SMI, or other earmarked trust funds for use in future decades, and if, in addition, that accumulation produced a net increase in total wealth to be available for retirement and personal care expenses at a later date. The OASI, DI, and HI (OASDHI) Trust Funds are used to purchase U.S. government securities only; nevertheless, when OASDHI revenues contribute to an overall budget surplus, the OASDHI funds can be used to retire federal debt, freeing private funds for investment in productive capital. By this route, payroll taxes can lead to an accumulation of private wealth. If, however, government instead takes advantage of a current-year trust fund expansion to fund deficit spending elsewhere in the budget, then no private funds are displaced, no additional capital investment is induced, and no real saving for the future is accomplished.

Table 5.1 shows how sizable recent accumulations by the OASDHI Trust Funds have been dwarfed by even larger deficits in the remainder of the federal budget. In 1989, for example, the OASDI and HI Trust Funds grew by $53 billion and $17 billion, respectively, but government securities purchased with these funds were completely absorbed by a deficit of $204 bil-

TABLE 5.1
Recent OASDHI Surpluses Compared to Overall
Federal Budget Deficits ($ Billions)

Calendar Year	Changes in Trust Fund Balances			Overall Federal Budget Deficit	Federal Budget Deficit Net of OASDHI Surplus
	OASI	DI	HI		
1984	7	−1	3	−170	−179
1985	9	2	5	−197	−213
1986	3	2	20	−207	−232
1987	23	−1	14	−158	−194
1988	41	0	16	−142	−199
1989	52	1	17	−134	−204
1990	59	3	13	−161ᴾ	−236

Source: Council of Economic Advisors (1991a), table B-79; and Social Security Administration, June 1991, tables M-4, M-5, and M-6.
Note: p = preliminary.

lion in the remainder of the budget. Excluding OASDHI, federal deficits have hovered around $200 billion (about 5% of 1989 GNP) throughout the 1980s. This massive structural deficit dates back to the personal income tax cuts enacted in the Reagan administration's first term. In order to replace lost income tax revenues, the Treasury has essentially borrowed OASDHI payroll tax revenues, rendering them unavailable to displace private investment funds. In fact, even the substantial OASDHI surpluses in 1988, 1989, and 1990 were sufficient to finance only about one-third of the deficit in the remainder of the budget, so that massive amounts of private funds also had to be borrowed each year to finance current federal spending.

The experience of the 1980s demonstrates the vulnerability of national saving, needed in the early twenty-first century to meet expanding retirement and health-care needs, to government dissaving: unfortunately, government deficits in other budget areas can more than offset any contribution of trust fund accumulation to national saving. Yet, in the 1980s, the Gramm-Rudman-Hollings legislation, requiring compliance with annual budget targets, focused attention on balancing the overall budget rather than the budget net of OASDHI accumulation. Trust fund surpluses have made the budget appear to be

closer to balance than it really was, perhaps moderating or preventing spending cuts or tax increases that might otherwise
have occurred.

For this reason, critics have charged that recent OASDHI
payroll tax increases, intended to fund future benefits, have
simply displaced personal income taxes, partially replacing a
progressive tax with a regressive tax. One of the most vocal of
these, U.S. Senator Daniel Patrick Moynihan (D-NY), has proposed legislation that would reduce OASDI payroll tax rates
and return the funding of those two programs to a pay-as-you-
go basis (National Academy of Social Insurance 1990).

The direct effect of this legislation on federal spending
would be to bring the OASDI portion of the budget closer to
balance, while worsening the imbalance in the overall budget.
The hoped-for indirect effect would be to encourage a greater
effort to balance the non-OASDI budget by making the size of
its deficit more apparent. The net result would be redistribution between birth cohorts: in the short term, current income
tax rates would have to be increased (or current spending reduced), in order to offset the effects of payroll tax cuts. In the
long term, the lower Treasury obligations to the trust funds
under pay-as-you-go would avert future personal income tax increases, but require payroll tax increases instead, as Baby
Boomers retire between 2010 and 2030. Shifts between payroll
and income taxation would by themselves produce no change
in overall government borrowing, however, and therefore, no
likely change of any consequence in the rate of private capital
accumulation.

Only if social insurance budgets are effectively excluded in
the setting of balanced-budget targets can government become
a net saver, rather than a borrower, and use accumulated trust
funds for their intended purpose, which is to provide a cushion
in a time of fiscal stress, such as the coming demographic transition. And it is not enough merely to set appropriate targets:
government must also meet those targets, actually living
within its means without dipping into public retirement and
health-care savings. Adequate trust fund accumulation is inex-
tricably linked with other fiscal policy, and will require very
large increases in overall federal taxation or reductions in over-

all federal expenditures in order to be effective in easing twenty-first century health-care financing burdens.

Greater Cost-Sharing: Claimants as Partners in Cost Control

At the same time that we seek new revenues with which to fund Medicare and other health-care programs, we could also look for ways to shift more of the burden of care to claimants, reducing public expenditures. If increased cost-sharing can be targeted toward elective care, it can reduce the moral hazard effect of Medicare, slowing the growth in demand for health care. What is least attractive about cost-sharing is that it saves at the expense of those currently experiencing health problems, whereas tax increases allow increased financial burdens to be distributed according to ability to pay. Since most of the elderly have backup coverage for Medicare's deductibles and coinsurance through either private medigap policies or Medicaid, however, much of the burden of greater Medicare cost-sharing would eventually be reflected in higher medigap premiums and personal income taxes rather than out-of-pocket expenses. The group most at risk from increased cost-sharing would be those who feel they cannot afford supplemental insurance but are also not poor enough to qualify for Medicaid.

Since the demand for outpatient care is more price-elastic than for inpatient care, there is greater potential for increased patient copayments to reduce costs for SMI than for HI. Moreover, HI's deductibles and coinsurance are already automatically increased every year in the same proportion as prospective payment rates, whereas Congress only increases the SMI deductible on an infrequent, ad hoc basis: it remained fixed at $75 from 1982 through 1990, for example. During this period, as physician's fees increased, more and more enrollees requiring only routine care exceeded the $75 deductible and faced a coinsurance rate of only 20% for any additional care that they sought. As a consequence, the average amount reimbursed by SMI per allowed medical bill actually fell between 1982 and 1990, from $52.1 to $50.79, at the same time that the number of SMI medical reimbursements increased by a factor of 2 ½.[2]

SMI's annual deductible was already $50 in 1966, when the program began operation. Consumer prices have more than tripled since 1966, and so have the Social Security benefits of those who were already collecting in 1966.[3] So it would be consistent with the original design of SMI to increase the deductible even beyond its current level of $100 to $150, and that figure could be price-indexed in subsequent years.

The coinsurance rate could also be raised for noncatastrophic SMI claims. A hypothetical SMI reimbursement schedule, incorporating a $150 deductible and initially higher coinsurance rates, is presented in table 5.2. Those with expenditures below $500 would face a 40% coinsurance rate, giving them greater incentive to economize on routine visits, while lower marginal coinsurance rates of 20% and 10% would be reserved for more catastrophic expenses. Those with $150 of reimbursements would be required to spend $40 more out-of-pocket than under current law. This difference would gradually increase to $110 for those with expenditures of $500, and then would remain constant over a broad 20% bracket: anyone with expenditures between $500 and $5000 would spend $110 more out-of-pocket than under current law. But for those whose costs exceeded $5000, the marginal share of costs borne out-of-pocket would be set lower than under current law; this would produce a crossover point where total cost reaches $6100, because at this point out-of-pocket costs under both the hypothetical plan and current law would be $1300. In the Medicare Castastrophic Coverage Act, out-of-pocket costs under SMI were to have been limited to a $1370 maximum. This hypothetical plan would provide some relief at roughly the same cat-

TABLE 5.2
Hypothetical and Actual SMI Reimbursement Schedules

Total Reimbursable SMI Cost ($)	Hypothetical Schedule		Actual Schedule	
	Marginal Coinsurance Rate (%)	Out-of-Pocket Cost ($)	Marginal Coinsurance Rate (%)	Out-of-Pocket Cost ($)
0–100	100	0–100	100	0–100
100–150	100	100–150	20	100–110
150–500	40	150–290	20	110–180
500–5000	20	290–1190	20	180–1080
5000–6100	10	1190–1300	20	1080–1300
6100–	10	1300–	20	1300–

astrophic threshold, reducing out-of-pocket costs below those imposed by current law and reducing the coinsurance rate on additional expenditure from 20% to 10%.

For those SMI enrollees whose copayments are covered by supplemental insurance, such a change would merely increase their insurer's liability at low and moderate levels of annual claims and decrease it at high levels. But this in itself would reduce SMI's costs; in addition, the resulting increases in medigap premiums would tend to reduce demand for coverage. If permitted by law, private insurers might also choose to cover less than the full coinsurance rate (40% in this example) in the lowest bracket. Either change, in premiums or in coverage, would indirectly reduce SMI's moral hazard problem.

Insurance vouchers are another proposal that would rely on consumer and insurer responses to changes in incentives. Instead of current SMI coverage, enrollees would be issued vouchers with which to purchase private insurance coverage or enroll in HMOs. Private insurers then would design reimbursement schedules as they saw fit; those who were most successful in reducing moral hazard among their enrolled population would be able to offer consumers the most for their money and would prosper. The consumer's incentive to carefully shop for the best insurance buy would arise out of the lump-sum nature of the voucher: every dollar saved on insurance premiums would be a dollar made available for other consumption, as long as the value of vouchers was set slightly below market premiums. If moral hazard were reduced, medical spending would fall, enabling the values of vouchers to be set below the current average level of reimbursement per SMI enrollee, so that program cost savings could be achieved. Vouchers would also give individuals the freedom to choose coverage consistent with their own personal taste for risk avoidance.

The lower the face value of the vouchers, the greater would be program cost savings. The consumer's incentive to shop around for insurance would be unaffected by variations in the size of the voucher, so that government could achieve any desired cost-saving within the framework of a voucher system, but some would doubtless forgo private insurance coverage altogether if the face value of vouchers were especially small.

The most serious drawback of vouchers is their vulnerability to adverse selection. Unless holders of vouchers could be accurately classified by risk class, with premiums set accordingly, poorer risks would be a threat to bankrupt any insurer offering fair coverage to the average customer. But this in turn would require a scaling of vouchers according to risk class. Use of age and sex as risk classifiers would likely violate antidiscrimination statutes and would be crude indicators in any case. A voucher system would also require recipients to assimilate a great deal of detailed information about available plans, in order to shop effectively. It would further require additional regulatory oversight of insurers, in order to prevent such abuses as low-option plans offering rebates to consumers, and would forfeit Medicare's market advantage as monopsony purchaser of outpatient care for the elderly, resulting in higher prices (Luft 1984).

The experience of the Federal Employees Health Benefits Program (FEHBP) is instructive, because it is the rough equivalent of a mandatory voucher system: employees are offered a choice between competing health plans, and must contribute a larger share of the premium the higher the plan's cost per enrollee. The experience of FEHBP, described in Chapter 4, has been for individual plans to go through life cycles, offering low premiums to generally young initial enrollees, with inertia preventing immediate enrollment by senior workers, and low-cost plans eventually becoming high-cost plans, unable to attract new members as enrollees age.

The coexistence of high- and low-cost plans under FEHBP suggests that it is costly for consumers to stay well-informed about changes in the menu of available plans, so that many ignore lower-cost plans as they become available, leaving their coverage unchanged despite its rising cost. The informational requirements imposed on recipients by a Medicare voucher system could lead to a similar enrollment cycle. If so, a de facto stratification would be the result: the youngest old would tend to be covered by newly created plans, and the oldest old by higher-cost plans of older vintage. Unless the law permitted voucher amounts to increase with age, the result could be a shifting of costs from younger to older enrollees. In addition, the ability of a voucher system to reduce expenditures depends on consumers' readiness to seek coverage at the best available price; any inertia due to the cost of keeping informed about the market would limit that ability.

Rationing Insured Care

Another approach to reducing spending under Medicare and other public programs is to better target coverage toward the population in greatest need of publicly financed insurance, and toward those services that are most effective in alleviating suffering and sustaining life.

Those with the greatest need for Medicare coverage are those who would lack the resources to acquire substitute private insurance and who, because of their age, could no longer obtain substitute coverage through employment. Medicare reimbursements could be made subject to income and wealth tests, so those with sufficient resources to purchase private coverage would be expected to do so in place of Medicare. And the age of initial Medicare eligibility could be delayed, in tandem with the age of eligibility for unreduced OASI benefits, as greater longevity and improving health make longer careers possible. The normal retirement age for OASI will begin to gradually increase in the year 2000, from 65 to 66 by 2005, and to 67 by 2022, and it seems natural for the age of initial HI eligibility to increase according to the same schedule.

The objective would be to increase self-sufficiency by those who are able to provide private insurance for themselves, either because they can readily afford it or because they can continue working and obtain coverage as a fringe benefit. Exclusion of the affluent presumes the emergence of a private market substitute for Medicare, however; insurer concerns about adverse selection might prevent the emergence of actuarially fair individual coverage. And raising the eligibility age for HI would also increase the number of Social Security recipients who are uncovered by HI: for those who retire prior to the "normal" age of 65, reduced OASI benefits are available as early as age 62, but there is no early counterpart to HI. As OASI's age of normal retirement rises to 67, reduced OASI benefits will remain available at ages 65 and 66, but HI benefits at those ages would disappear if HI's age of initial eligibility were increased. Employer-provided insurance for the retired seems unlikely to expand sufficiently to fully offset the lost HI benefits, considering the unfunded liabilities already incurred by employers.

Rather than to selectively eliminate coverage, relying on individuals and employers to arrange private coverage, it may be preferable to continue to provide pooled coverage through HI but to require selected groups to pay toward their coverage. With regard to ability to pay, this could mean imposing an income-related premium on the highest-income HI enrollees; if maintaining a positive return to past HI payroll tax payments were to remain a goal of the program, any income-related premium would have to be set well below the voluntary premium paid by non-OASDHI–covered enrollees. HI coverage for those retiring before age 67, after it has become the normal retirement age for OASI, could be maintained without cost to HI by making HI coverage mandatory between ages 65 and 67 for those claiming OASI benefits before age 67, but deducting a premium (for example, in the same amount as the voluntary premium) from OASI checks. This would be a significant new incentive to avoid early retirement, and yet early retirees would experience no reduction in coverage due to the change. For workers who were physically unable to continue work until 67 and qualified for Disability Insurance (which is essentially equivalent to OASI with unreduced benefits), HI could remain available without a premium, as it is today for all DI beneficiaries.

Increasing attention has also been paid to the possibility of curtailing care for the oldest, possibly through age limits on Medicare or other insurance reimbursements, because medical care may have the least potential to sustain a long and satisfying life at the oldest ages. A number of influential academic observers and public officials (Daniels 1983 and 1988; Callahan 1987; Lamm 1984) have argued that it may be just, under some circumstances, to limit the care that we provide to older Americans. In the public arena, then-Governor Lamm (1984) of Colorado asserted that "we all have a duty to die," that is, that timely death is a duty of every individual to society. Aaron and Schwartz (1984) have highlighted elements of age rationing in the British National Health system, a system that absorbs a much smaller part of national product than the U.S. system.

Callahan (1987) has explored the obligations of government to provide care, and has argued that government has a duty "to help people live out a normal life span," but that beyond that point its resources should be used only to relieve suffering, not to extend life. Daniels (1983, 1988) has argued that rationing health care according to the age of the patient may be justified, even though rationing may reduce the chance of living a "longer-than-normal lifespan," because it frees resources for the saving of lives of younger people, increasing the chances of reaching a "normal lifespan." Battin (1987) has even gone a step further, argumentatively asserting that "direct-killing" or the encouragement of suicide at the onset of a professionally determined "terminal downhill course" would be more efficient, in the sense that even more resources would be freed for promoting the survival of the young than are freed when care is simply withheld.

Daniels (1983, 1988) has proposed a way of thinking about justice in distributing resources across age groups by considering the point of view of what he calls a "prudent deliberator." This hypothetical decision maker must prospectively allocate a limited budget of resources over a lifetime and does not have foreknowledge of his or her future personal circumstances in life, but is aware of general economic, demographic, and social trends. The prudent deliberator's goal is to "assure a fair chance at enjoyment of the normal opportunity range for each life-stage." Daniels reasons that such a person would devote substantial resources to health care at younger ages, since at those ages the most potential exists for many more years of life and for the future fulfillment of one's life plans. This would make resources scarcer later in life, and the most prudent available method for living within one's tightened lifetime budget constraint might be age rationing. Put another way, age rationing is something that each of us might choose voluntarily but for the knowledge of our individual circumstances of health and for the shortening of our planning period as we make a one-way passage through the life cycle.

A reader may conclude that justice dictates age rationing of health care in the twenty-first century, as the work force shrinks relative to the aged population, in order to maintain the flow of adequate health care and other necessary goods and services to the nonaged. But the squaring of the age pyramid reduces lifetime budgets only to the extent that intergenerational transfers are the means chosen to meet retirement needs: if the prudent deliberator transfers his or her own resources from youth to old age, then his or her lifetime budget is not directly affected by the size of the labor force. In particular, a prudent deliberator beginning life in the twenty-first century, facing a demographic environment very different from that of the mid-twentieth century, could expand his or her lifetime budget by choosing a funded system of retirement and health-care financing; one would be imprudent to rule out saving when the payroll tax base is growing slowly. Thus, age rationing in future decades arguably flows from Daniels's thought-experiment only as a second-best solution, if fund accumulation fails. To focus solely on rationing limited resources is to ignore the means by which resource constraints can be relaxed, namely, the accumulation of funds to provide for the future.

The prudence of reallocating resources from old to young also depends on the relative effectiveness of resources in promoting health and survival at each age, and in this regard two further cautions about age rationing are in order. First, as with any other undertaking, progress in preventing premature death is increasingly costly, the more intensively society devotes resources to that task. According to the economic principle of diminishing marginal returns, there is a point beyond which we obtain less and less additional output per additional unit of resources applied to the production of that output. When we use medical resources to promote the survival of the young, the benefits of additional care must decline as care is provided in less and less promising ways. Considerable resources are already devoted to the survival of younger people; much of the remaining loss of life prior to old age may only be preventable by nonmedical means and at great cost. Work-related stress, exposure to environmental hazards, accidental trauma, homicide, and substance abuse all reduce the chance of survival, regardless of medical expenditures. We should not assume its cost to be low, relative to the cost of sustaining life at older ages.

Second, improved care for the young would be only one of many competing uses for resources made available by denying care to some on the basis of age. The denial of Medicare or other reimbursements to the oldest old would leave taxpayers with more after-tax income to spend, and with the right to spend it as they do their other income, on a wide variety of goods and services. In the long run, as demand for those other goods increased, the capital displaced by the age rationing of care could be devoted to other products altogether, and workers not needed to care for the elderly could be trained and employed from the beginnings of their careers in entirely different professions. Surely many of the resources saved would not be devoted to health care at all. The argument for age-rationing seems morally compelling when the outcome is argued to be longer lives for healthy people, but is much less so to the extent that the gain would be expanded production of ordinary consumer products.

In any case, individual lifetime budget constraints will tighten in the twenty-first century only if the aged are supported and insured by transfers from others; with sufficient increases in the rate of saving, lifetime budgets would be protected from changes in the age pyramid and the age rationing of care made unnecessary.

Alternative Financing of Long-Term-Care Services

As documented in Chapter 3, most long-term-care services are financed out-of-pocket or through Medicaid. Medicaid's reimbursement limits and state rationing of certificates of need have led to shortages of beds and to concerns about quality of care. Restrictions on the type of care reimbursed have also promoted excessive institutionalization, and means tests have required impoverishment as a precondition for assistance. Because Medicaid requires no cost-sharing (such as by families) beyond the spending-down of the beneficiary's resources, Medicaid provides little incentive for users to minimize program costs. And, in part because Medicaid exists as a fallback, private long-term coverage has been slow to develop, making it difficult for consumers to soften the blow of unexpected out-of-pocket outlays by pooling risk.

The following four sections discuss alternative means of financing long-term care which would address these problems, including the reorganization of Medicaid, its replacement with mandatory public or private coverage, a more rational integration of family and institutional care, and the promotion of innovative forms of voluntary private coverage.

Changes in the Structure of Medicaid

Current law requires the federal government to match state Medicaid spending according to a formula based on a state's average per capita income. The statutory minimum federal contribution is 50% of program costs, and the percentage is about 80% in the lowest-income states.[4] As the major contributor of funds, the federal government retains authority over the scope of state Medicaid programs, requiring certain coverages (such as hospital and physician services) and limiting optional coverage to a list of 32 services (such as intermediate care services for the aged but excluding custodial care). But the preponderance of federal matching funds also weakens the resolve of the individual states to control costs, within the range of programs allowed by federal guidelines: a state paying as little as 20% of the cost of care has little incentive to monitor the need for or cost-effectiveness of that care.

An alternative method of financing Medicaid would be to provide states with block grants instead of matching funds. These grants could be allotted according to state income, as matching funds are under the current system. As a condition of the block grant, states would be required to provide certain basic coverage, but beyond that coverage they would be permitted to include any other services appropriate to that individual state's needs and preferences. Bearing the full marginal cost of additional services would promote greater cost-consciousness by the states, even while allowing them greater program flexibility, creating an opportunity for the federal contribution to Medicaid to be reduced. In fact, the elimination of the subsidy to marginal spending, brought about by the introduction of a block grant system, would increase the relative importance of an incentive working in the opposite direction, associated with migration. States with the lowest benefits would expect to attract the fewest immigrants in need of Medicaid services and to experience the greatest rate of immigration by the Medicaid users. Because this externality would tend to drive benefits below otherwise desirable levels without net savings for the United States as a whole, the setting of minimum standards by the federal government would be important in insuring the adequacy of Medicaid coverage.

A variant that would attempt to further improve the match between needs and services would be to channel all funds for long-term care, as currently provided through Medicare, Medicaid, Title XX, and local agencies into a block grant to a single local agency, called a local-area management organization (LAMO) by Ruchlin et al. (1982). The current fragmentation of funding tends to channel care recipients into skilled, intermediate, custodial, or home care based on their program eligibility, whereas the LAMO, with responsibility as "gate-keeper, case-manager, quality-of-care assessor, and purchaser of care," would be freer to choose appropriate services for each individual client.

Medicaid rules could also be modified to promote long-term care insurance coverage among the low- and moderate-income elderly. Where long-term-care insurance has an upper limit on the length of a covered stay, the insured faces the prospect of spending down income and wealth to qualify for Medicaid, rendering the private coverage of little value. Instead, those paying for long-term care with private insurance, for some minimum time such as three years, could be offered protection against subsequent Medicaid spend-down, in order to make coverage more attractive. And Medicaid could also pay long-term-care insurance premiums for low-income eligible persons, in order to expand the risk pool and make coverage more viable (Meiners 1988).

Mandatory Long-Term-Care Insurance

The goal of block grants and more centralized administration would be to streamline and improve the targeting of care to the long-term-care population currently served by public programs. This would do little, however, to serve those who do not currently qualify for long-term-care assistance under public programs but are also poorly served by the private insurance market. Those who are at risk to pay the entire cost of long-term care out of pocket would be better served by the introduction of mandatory long-term-care insurance, either through a single social insurance program or provided by private insurance vendors.

Mandatory coverage would eliminate some of the problems that have inhibited the growth of private insurance coverage. Most important, adverse selection would be avoided. In addition, the availability of Medicaid to those who spend down income and wealth has weakened the market for voluntary insurance, increasing the likelihood of impoverishment for those developing long-term-care needs; mandatory insurance would take most long-term-care coverage out of the welfare system, while still allowing for special treatment of the poor, such as through income-related copayments and subsidies to premiums. The most important concern in such a massive expansion of the insured population is increased utilization of services, since the out-of-pocket price of care would be greatly reduced for the bulk of the eligible population which does not currently qualify for Medicaid.

Administrative costs would be lowest if mandatory coverage were extended through uniform nationwide social insurance, which might be called "Medicare Part C." Administrative efficiencies would arise not only out of scale economies but also from the use of the preexisting Medicare apparatus to minimize start-up costs. The avoidance of margins for selling commissions and profits would also help to keep premiums low.

The replacement of Medicaid's long-term-care function by a new Medicare component would reduce the burden on the states of financing long-term care but would shift that burden onto the new federal program. Of total Medicaid payments of $54.5 billion in 1989, only $34.5 billion were paid for by the federal government,[5] and the difference represents the state share that would have to be replaced, even if the new program produced no change in utilization. To raise the needed additional funds, an increment to either the Medicare payroll tax or a new premium would be needed, and the new premium would be preferable in that it would ease the financing burden of the Baby Boom's ultimate long-term-care needs: an actuarially fair premium would produce an accumulation of funds, even if premiums were not collected until age 65, because long-term-care needs are highly concentrated in later years of life.

Public long-term-care insurance would raise the same design issues as other insurance, and its financial viability would largely depend on the choices made and their effects on moral

hazard and utilization. Most important, there is the definition
of the insurable event: if institutionalization or a high intensity
of care are prerequisites for reimbursement, then the impaired
will be induced to seek such care (Leutz and Greenberg 1985).
The alternative, which risks bringing substantial numbers of
lower intensity cases "out of the woodwork" for assistance by
the public program, would be to determine eligibility based on
disability, rather than current utilization of services. A prototype plan proposed by Bishop (1981), for example, would use
panels of professionals to make yes-no disability determina-
tions and allow individuals to choose their own services, relying on beneficiary copayments to minimize overutilization. Or,
instead of service benefits with copayment requirements,
claimants could be issued cash or a voucher in an amount
scaled according to the nature of the disability. Either copayments or vouchers would rely on consumer shopping to obtain
the most economical and appropriate care available within a
fixed budget.

Bishop also proposed a deductible for institutional care,
equal to SSI's food and housing allowance; to omit such a "basic living needs" deductible would perpetuate the market-
basket bias toward institutionalization caused by Medicaid's
full reimbursement for institutional care. A high coinsurance
rate would help to finance the program and to reduce moral
hazard, encouraging the impaired to use less costly home and
informal care when possible. Even with a coinsurance rate as
high as one-third, the majority of nursing home residents who
now pay for care out-of-pocket would be made much better off.
The disadvantage of substantial coinsurance is that the most
afflicted are required to pay for a large share of the program,
subverting its insurance objective. An additional layer of protection could be added by establishing a floor below which income net of copayments could not fall, and by making that
floor high enough to guarantee families more protected income
than the small amounts allowed under current Medicaid
spend-down requirements.

The potential for moral hazard in providing home-based
services that are purely custodial is probably so great as to pre-
clude them from any expanded social insurance program. More
generally, any expansion of coverage of home-based care is

likely to be enormously expensive, because of the large potential pool of partially disabled clients, unless coverage with low copayments can be limited to those for whom such care is medically necessary.

Alternatively, universal long-term-care insurance could be provided without expanding the public sector by mandating private coverage. Both mandatory auto insurance coverage and workers' compensation programs are important precedents at the state level, in that each uses the private insurance system to guarantee coverage for a class of physical impairments.

An advantage of mandatory private coverage over an alternative social insurance program is that mandatory private insurance standards could be written broadly enough to permit individuals some choice between alternative coverages, especially with regard to treatment setting. The choice of institutional care versus home care is often a matter of strong personal preference, even given one's disability status and living arrangement, and to provide uniform institutional- or home-care coverage, as in a single public program, would require some to insure for services they would prefer not to choose, and would even induce some to use those less-preferred services for lack of their preferred coverage.

Adequate provision for those with limited resources would have to be made in mandating private coverage. Since those who are poor prior to disability are hard-pressed to pay either premiums or copayments, it would be appropriate to retain the public assistance function currently performed by Medicaid for the low-income aged. The likelihood of spending-down to Medicaid could be curbed, however, by requiring private policies to meet minimum coverage standards, such as maximum deductibles and coinsurance rates.

Like voucher plans, mandatory private insurance would place on consumers the heavy informational burden that necessarily accompanies freedom of choice. The burden is less pressing in purchasing insurance than in purchasing acute care since there is less hurry to initiate the transaction; still, survey evidence of policyholder misconceptions about current medigap coverage warns us to beware of the difficulty consumers face in translating their insurance preferences into coverage. Bishop (1981) has proposed the introduction of consumer advocates, public servants who would promote the flow of information about coverage, but acknowledges that it may be difficult to administratively shield the consumer advocates from regulatory and budgetary authorities. Conflicts between the interests of insurers, taxpayers, and insurance consumers could make the role of the neutral provider of information difficult to play.

And free choice among insurance offerings also risks adverse selection: while different coverages may serve subpopulations with different preferences for type of care, they are also likely to be differentially appealing to consumers with different health histories and perceived long-term-care risks. This would tend to increase the cost of coverage by clustering those with high risks for certain losses in coverages which generously reimburse for those losses. This disadvantage of decentralized coverage must be weighed against the benefits of greater consumer sovereignty and any cost-saving forced on insurers by competition for customers.

Integrating Public Programs with Family Care

Medicaid's encouragement of costly institutionalization, in cases where less formal care would be just as efficacious, results in a highly visible burden on taxpayers. The apparent corollary is that liberalized reimbursement for home and community-based care could reduce the cost of care without a loss of services to those who need them. But most care is already provided informally, outside of institutions: Doty (1986) reports that about three-fourths of the functionally disabled elderly are cared for solely by family members, compared to about one-fifth in nursing homes, and that most of the remainder are cared for by a combination of family members and paid helpers. The importance of family will be even greater in the twenty-first century: in fact, greater than fivefold increases, between 1980 and 2040, in care needed from spouses and offspring have been projected by Manton and Soldo (1985). Therein lies the danger inherent in liberalization of home care: an effort to substitute informal care for institutional care risks also displacing the assistance of families, increasing the number of elderly dependent upon the state for care. And to make assistance available only to those who cannot turn to close relatives for help risks undermining family ties.

The potential for the disruption of family support is akin to that faced by Aid to Families of Dependent Children (AFDC), a program originally designed to provide support to children of single, full-time homemakers. As Murray (1984) has charged, making AFDC assistance contingent on marital and employment status may discourage marriage and market employment. In the same way, restricting home care reimbursement to those lacking family help, or offsetting potential family help against available public assistance on anything approaching a dollar-for-dollar or hour-for-hour basis, would encourage families to abandon their elders to the state. Yet home care reimbursement for the elderly would be extraordinarily expensive if offered to all who are now provided for by families at home.

Consider, for example, the proposal by Callahan et al. (1980), to add to Medicaid's eligibility procedures an additional determination of the amount of informal home care services to be required of spouses, children, and other relatives, given household and family structure, as an in-kind copayment toward Medicaid assistance. While this would doubtless leave many supportive family situations unaltered, it also could induce some to reside at a distance from disabled elders, or to renounce legal responsibility in whatever other way would be necessary to avoid obligation for in-kind copayments.

The challenge that public programs face in taking proper account of family resources is to avoid subsidizing abandonment by treating the families of the abandoned elderly no more or less favorably than supportive families. The analogy with AFDC is instructive: a certainty of child-support obligations for biological fathers, whether or not they are married to their child's mother, could reduce any incentive for potential AFDC mothers to remain single, for then marriage would be irrelevant to the counting of the father's contributions to the family against AFDC eligibility. Analogously, any family copayment toward long-term-care assistance should ideally be inescapable by those with close financial ties to the beneficiary. An inheritance tax surcharge would be one way to retroactively bill any heirs for long-term-care copayments previously evaded by obscuring dependency relationships.

Any proposal to require family copayments could strive for neutrality between family and institutional care by requiring comparable family contributions, regardless of setting. The alternative to copayments which would also be neutral with respect to family status is to reimburse families for the care they provide, just as Medicare now reimburses professional care providers. Because of the vast amount of care already provided by families, however, such reimbursement would be enormously expensive. Families who provide only in-kind services to their elders currently receive no such federal assistance. The federal Dependent Care Credit, allowed against personal income taxes, provides some reimbursement to family members who pay for a dependent's care, but only to the extent that it frees them for employment, and it comes to much less than the full cost of care.

Tax credits and direct payments are expensive windfalls to those family members who would provide help even without them. Nor do most families who care for disabled relatives appear to view direct financial aid as the most appropriate form of government assistance. A survey of primary-care-giving relatives currently receiving home- or day-care services in New York City (Horowitz and Shindelman 1983) asked each to identify the public supports they considered most critical to sustaining care-giving efforts. In-kind medical and home-making services were cited much more frequently than either direct payments or preferential tax treatment, and fully 26% refused to complete the section on economic incentives, many of them registering offense at the survey questions. The authors concluded that time and emotional resources are scarcer than money in care-giving households, so that in-kind assistance, freeing family members to take care of other responsibilities, would be more effective than cash in bolstering the resolve of families to provide care at home.

Maintaining help from families at its currently high level would be essential to the success of any social insurance program providing home nursing care services. Family deductibles for publicly reimbursed care, structured in such a way that they could be met with a certain number of hours worked by family members, could be used as the stick to promote family care, but if so, modest in-kind assistance to families probably would also be an effective carrot. Copayments would also help keep program expenditures down but would have to strive for neutrality with respect to care setting, in order to minimize institutional bias and, above all with respect to family configuration, in order to minimize abandonment. Only if a workable way can be found to impose copayments on those who would disavow responsibility for their elders, such as through inheritance taxation, would it be sound policy to impose long-term-care obligations on family members.

Saving and Insurance Innovations

The Social/Health Maintenance Organization. Because of the difficulty of limiting care in informal settings, Medicare and Medicaid, and much of the private insurance that is available, limit coverage to brief recoveries from acute episodes. As a result, long-term care is inadequately insured, and too often provided in expensive formal settings. Little insurance exists that can help an aged person maintain an independent life in the community; if such assistance is not available from local agencies, it may be necessary under current arrangements for a person in need of care to enter a nursing home, often at government expense. The Social/Health Maintenance Organization (S/HMO) is an innovative arrangement that attempts to solve this problem by insuring long-term care as part of a package which integrates delivery of acute and long-term-care services with other community social support services. Like HMOs, care is prepaid under S/HMOs, so that the provider is also the insurer.

The S/HMO model, as embodied in four mid-1980s demonstration projects, includes in its service package acute inpatient care, diagnostic and ancillary services, outpatient medical and social service visits, therapeutic services, skilled nursing home and intermediate care services, home health services, optometry, homemaker services, prescription drugs, counseling, emergency mental health, and transportation services. The federal government has provided Medicare program waivers to the S/HMO demonstrations enabling Medicare enrollees to substitute S/HMO coverage for conventional Medicare coverage; waiving the usual patient copayments, Medicare has reimbursed the demonstration S/HMOs for 100% of its avoided hospital and physician costs, estimated by local area. The long-term-care portion of the S/HMO has been financed by Medicaid, by Title XX, and by copayments and supplemental enrollee premiums. Membership is voluntary and limited to the aged population. Because of the wide range of services, many may be contracted out to other providers, in contrast to the centralization of HMOs (Diamond and Berman 1981).

The potential advantages of S/HMOs over fragmented provision of care are improved case management and the promotion of economy by limiting the budget available to the provider. By coordinating services, S/HMOs can facilitate the substitution of appropriate home- and community-based care for inpatient care, and can take advantage of economies of scale in administration and case management. By giving the insurer direct control over provision of long-term care, they aim to minimize the moral hazard problem with regard to those services that substitute for ordinary living costs or for informal services already provided by family members. If the S/HMO is successful in providing low-cost coverage, it has great promise as a vehicle for expanding long-term-care coverage. Cohen et al. (1987) found that a greater proportion of the elderly could afford S/HMO coverage than long-term-care insurance, and a much greater proportion than could afford fees for Continuing Care Retirement Communities. In addition, an orientation toward health maintenance, as in conventional HMOs, may lessen the need for long-term care through early detection and treatment of chronic illness.

While a capitated arrangement enhances the incentives for providers to limit services, it does not guarantee that they will develop the technical means to do so. This is an especially important concern with regard to nonprofessional home services, such as homemaker services. Without rationing, copayments, or queues, S/HMOs are just as likely as conventional insurers to suffer from overconsumption of covered home services (Diamond and Berman 1981).

But the power to prevent overconsumption also presents a danger that needs may be underserved by providers, especially if S/HMOs develop "bare bones" standards of practice, imposed by nonclinicians rather than professional management on the physician model. Peer review, external audits, and the availability of grievance procedures could be employed as safeguards. And tying the Medicare capitation rate to the S/HMO's case mix would lessen the danger that S/HMOs could attempt to avoid providing costly services by "creaming" the lowest risks from an applicant population (Leutz 1986).

Forecasting costs for an innovative arrangement like the S/HMO is difficult: the extent of adverse selection, the extent to which pioneer S/HMOs would be able to prevent overconsumption of services, and the relation between the size of the risk pool and the variation in costs were all unknown at the outset of the S/HMO demonstrations. The federal and state governments have shared these risks in the demonstration S/HMOs by providing aggregate stop-loss insurance on total plan losses and gains, and in return have required plans to enroll populations that are no more or less chronically ill than the aged community at large. Several of the plans have accomplished this by accepting or assigning applicants to waiting lists, depending upon their levels of impairment (Greenberg, Leutz, and Abrahams 1985), and this appears to have been an effective way to achieve the enrollment of an S/HMO population very much like the community's overall older population (Greenberg et al. 1988). After plan experience is better established, S/HMOs will be expected to bear the full risk of unexpectedly high expenses; to allow otherwise would weaken their incentive to economize, putting the government at risk of subsidizing an overconsumption of insured expenses. If queuing methods ultimately prove inadequate to establish a balanced risk pool, it may be necessary for S/HMOs to establish differential reimbursement rates, based on applicants' impairment levels and associated actuarial risks (Diamond and Berman 1981).

Market surveys indicate that the breadth of coverage offered by S/HMOs is a plus, greatly simplifying the enrollees' informational requirements in obtaining care. But marketing considerations also imposed limits on the demonstration S/HMOs: in order to keep premiums close to those required by conventional SMI coverage, less-than-full long-term-care coverage has been offered (Greenberg, Leutz, and Abrahams 1985).

Marketing turned out to be a problem for the demonstration S/HMOs, keeping enrollment well below expectations at three out of four sites; Greenberg et al (1988) speculate that some consumers may have mistakenly delayed enrollment until the onset of chronic illness, unaware that the disabled were placed on waiting lists, as this queuing arrangement was not widely publicized.

S/HMOs could be spawned by existing HMOs, Preferred Provider Insurance plans (PPIs), or Individual Practice Associations (IPAs). A related possibility is the emergence of joint ventures linking Medicare HMOs and private long-term-care insurers (Hughes 1986). Such mergers would enable HMOs to expand their provision of long-term care beyond the limits set by Medicare and Medicaid reimbursement, while enabling insurers to market to groups rather than individuals, reducing adverse selection and promoting scale economies. Partnership with HMOs would also enable long-term-care insurers to more efficiently monitor benefit use.

Another structure around which S/HMOs could be built is a "channeling organization," a local agency with responsibility for coordination and delivery of long-term personal and social services. While channeling organizations lack the hospital facilities that HMOs can contribute to formation of an S/HMO, they would provide instead a network of provider relationships and expertise in substituting less formal care for institutional care (Diamond and Berman 1981).

But marketing evidence shows a consumer reluctance to experiment with the new arrangement unless it is presented as a variation on an existing institution, such as an established HMO. Although the lower investment requirements of PPI and IPA plans have enabled them to grow more rapidly in recent years than HMOs among the nonaged population (Enthoven 1987), the potential for savings through improved case management and scale economies is greater where services are provided under one roof than when they are contracted from a large number of providers. Thus, HMOs seem the stronger candidates to spawn S/HMOs. Further, studies of Medicare HMO experience show that they have achieved overall savings through reduced hospital admissions and length of stay, due in part to substitution of ambulatory and home health services (Diamond and Berman 1981). So far, demonstration experience does show those S/HMOs sponsored by HMOs to have fared better financially than those which are freestanding (Greenberg et al. 1988).

Because the S/HMO's greatest departures from current norms of coverage are in long-term care, the public program whose role would be most altered by the emergence of S/HMOs on a large scale is Medicaid, especially with regard to its spend-down provisions. Because of the improved coverage, some who under current arrangements would be forced to exhaust their resources and become Medicaid-eligible would instead, as S/HMO members, be able to obtain long-term care without government help beyond the capitation paid by Medicare. Some of these savings could be directed toward subsidies of S/HMOs, possibly reducing required copayments for long-term services, thereby increasing the adequacy of insurance for the nonpoor and encouraging enrollment.

A significant expansion of the S/HMO safety net could also erode popular support for Medicaid coverage of the elderly; its natural constituency would no longer include all of those now vulnerable to impoverishment by catastrophic illness, only those who enter old age already in poverty. In this way, the proliferation of S/HMOs (or any other expansion of private insurance against long-term-care costs) might indirectly reduce the availability of all medical and long-term-care services to the poor, even while improving long-term-care coverage for middle-income families.

Continuing Care Retirement Communities. Even greater continuity of care is provided by Continuing Care Retirement Communities (CCRCs), sometimes called life-care facilities. These facilities provide residential living quarters and also long-term-care services when needed by residents. Many CCRCs offer those services on a capitated lifetime basis, so that they really insure against medical and long-term-care needs in the same way as the S/HMO, and in addition provide annuitized housing services. For more affluent older persons who own houses outright but have difficulty maintaining them, CCRCs provide a means to convert part of their home equity into personal care insurance and eliminate their responsibilities for upkeep, while retaining much of the sense of security that comes with homeownership. And CCRCs offer a sense of community to those who feel isolated in their homes.

Entrance into CCRCs is contingent upon payment of a substantial entrance fee; subsequent monthly service charges are sufficient to retain a lifetime claim to services, but some CCRCs also require copayments for nursing services, often after a guaranteed number of days per year of free care. These fees are combined by CCRCs with reimbursements from Medicare, Medicaid, and private insurance to finance the complete package. While most CCRCs combine residence and nursing facilities on a single site, some are simply residences that contract for nursing services with independent nursing facilities.

Capitation provides incentives for cost-effective management in CCRCs just as in S/HMOs, at least with regard to services not reimbursible by public or private insurance. Nevertheless, most CCRCs enjoy a reputation for high quality care (Hughes 1986).

Like S/HMOs, CCRCs must confront the risk of adverse selection. The usual strategy is to screen applicants, admitting only the youngest and those in the best health. By doing so, CCRCs are able to keep the fraction of residents who use nursing services during their stay down to about 20% (Hughes 1986), and utilization through age 85 in CCRCs appears to be comparable to that of the general population of the same age (Cohen 1988).

An additional risk of CCRCs, to the extent that they are smaller than S/HMOs, is greater random year-to-year variation in utilization. And CCRC residents bear much more of the risk themselves than S/HMO members, because an insolvent CCRC would be unable to return the entrance fee, yet also unable to provide promised services. The fees charged by CCRCs have historically proven sufficient, so that there have been few failures (Leutz 1986). Nevertheless, Ruchlin (1988) has raised concern about the generally high debt-to-asset ratios and low net worth of those CCRCs that require only small copayments for nursing care.

While CCRCs are proliferating rapidly, they nevertheless occupy only a small market niche and remain inaccessible to all but the most affluent because of their high entrance fees; Cohen et al. (1987) find them affordable by fewer than 10% of the elderly. The promotion of increased private saving is crucial to the broadening of the CCRC's market base.

Adverse selection imposes a further limit on CCRC expansion: selling one's home and moving into a low-maintenance apartment unit becomes more attractive when disabilities begin to limit one's independence, yet disabilities are good predictors of high future nursing care utilization, reducing an applicant's chance of admission to a CCRC. Thus, the opportunity to move into a CCRC, requiring a permanent move, often passes before the young retired are really ready to make such a drastic change in lifestyle. A system of preenrollment might enable CCRCs to appeal to a larger proportion of the young-old population. If newly retired persons could purchase the right to enter a CCRC at a fixed later date (possibly allowing for earlier entry upon the death of a spouse), with funds kept in an escrow account for their protection until that date, then CCRC enrollment might be just as attractive for healthy persons who expect to eventually need care as it is to those who can no longer live independently. For homeowners without sufficient liquid funds to prepay an entrance fee, home equity conversion (see below) offers a way to guarantee CCRC entrance without moving out of one's home prematurely.

Another residential arrangement that provides for those who cannot live independently, but do not yet require the skilled services of a nursing home, is the board-and-care facility: these provide food, shelter, and other nonmedical services, charging residents a monthly fee for the whole package. Thus, except for nursing care, the board-and-care facility provides most of the same services as a CCRC. While a board-and-care resident with adequate long-term-care insurance would be nearly as well served as a CCRC resident, the CCRC's capitated funding arrangement promises more cost-effective care, and the residential continuity and annuitized housing services make the CCRC more attractive from a marketing standpoint.

Life Care at Home and Long-Life Insurance. A variant of the CCRC, providing similar long-term-care services but allowing subscribers to remain in their homes, has been proposed by Tell et al. (1987b), and is called Life Care at Home (LCAH). Like CCRCs, LCAH would require an entry fee and monthly payments and would both insure and manage long-term care, but unlike CCRCs LCAH would aim to provide it at lower cost by eliminating the campus setting. In order to manage risks, case workers would objectively determine eligibility for chronic care services, and benefits would be limited and subject to cost sharing. Adverse selection would be controlled by preenrollment screening. In a survey of those on two CCRC waiting lists, almost 40% expressed interest in LCAH and willingness to pay its estimated costs; for those who did not, concerns about social isolation and housekeeping were important in their preference for CCRCs.

Another model variant, called "Long-Life Insurance" (Getzen 1988), would limit adverse selection by combining LCAH coverage with an annuity payable 15 years after initial enrollment. Enrollees would thereby be insured against both chronic dependency and outliving one's resources, and the negative correlation between these risks would tend to reduce self-selection due to either risk alone.

Private Long-Term-Care Insurance. A drawback of the continuous care provided by S/HMOs and CCRCs is their restriction of choice by individuals: care for an S/HMO member is insured only if supplied by the S/HMO or its chosen provider, and the greater continuity of care in the CCRC is further tied to residence in that facility. Ideally, private long-term-care insurance policies combine greater flexibility with comparable coverage for long-term care.

The proportion of the elderly who "need significant formal or informal support" is as low as 10%–20%, according to Leutz and Greenberg (1985). And even among those admitted to nursing homes, there is a high variance in utilization: Liu and Manton (1983) found that fully 60% of admissions in one year were discharged in the same calendar year, but that these patients accounted for only 7% of patient days in that year. The low probability of a long spell of nursing care makes it an obvious candidate for risk pooling: actuarially fair premiums are much less costly for an individual than the accumulation of savings sufficient to pay the full cost of care. Sharing the cost of the longest spells of care among the majority who will never need them provides enhanced security for all participants.

Private coverage also reduces public transfers, especially Medicaid payments. About one in three Medicaid nursing home residents become eligible for Medicaid only after spending-down their assets, and for more than half the spend-down period exceeds six months (Meiners 1983). Expanded private insurance coverage extends an individual's ability to self-finance, prolonging the spend-down process and reducing the proportion of long-term care reimbursed by Medicaid. In addition, it puts the savings of each retiring generation to use in paying for its own growing long-term-care bill, moderating the need to impose higher tax rates on the incomes of less rapidly growing younger cohorts.

Until recently, what private coverage existed for institutionalized nursing care was very limited, and coverage for home-based care was quite rare. Wary that moral hazard would lead to overutilization, private insurers commonly required hospitalization prior to skilled nursing home care, skilled care prior to lower levels of care, and institutionalized nursing care prior to home care (Wilson and Weissert 1989). Maximum coverage periods generally declined with the level of skill required, reinforcing the public sector's bias toward highly skilled institutional care. Confusing (even to nursing care professionals) definitions of skilled, intermediate, and custodial care further complicated reimbursement (Weiner et al. 1987). And high premiums limited coverage to the more affluent (Leutz and Greenberg 1985); as recently as 1988, as few as 2% of the elderly were reported to have long-term-care insurance (Wallack 1988).

In the early 1980s, Meiners (1983) and Meiners and Trapnell (1984) provided cost estimates for a prototype plan providing coverage for a broader range of nursing home stays and also for home care. The subsequent response of the industry has been impressive: more than 100 insurance companies have responded by offering policies, increasing the number sold annually by a factor of 10 between 1986 and 1990. By 1991, more than 1.5 million policies had been sold in the United States (Consumers Union 1991).[6] While this number still represents only about one policy for every 20 citizens aged 65 or older, it is still a substantial increase.

In some ways, the actual offerings are more generous than the prototype that Meiners and Trapnell advocated. It included, for example, a 90-day deductible, or "waiting period," to discourage overutilization, based on the reasoning that nearly half of nursing home stays are for 90 days or fewer,[7] so that the savings to insurers (especially in administrative costs) would be substantial. In fact, waiting periods as short as 30 days are now usually offered, with longer waiting periods available as lower-premium options. Meiners and Trapnell also put a ceiling of three years on covered lengths of stay in order to limit insurer liability, reasoning that only about 15% of stays exceed this length, and that Medicaid would remain as an insurer of last resort in such cases. But most offer coverage for at least four years and some for a lifetime.

Coverage is typically granted for stays in either skilled or intermediate care facilities, and is contingent upon medical necessity due to sickness or injury or upon inability to perform specified activities of daily living. The requirement of prior hospitalization has been dropped from most policies.

In addition to the risk of disablement itself, the customer and insurer face the risk of inflation in the cost of services over the term of a potentially very long contract. This is a risk for which insurers have chosen to insure rather poorly: where inflation protection is offered (at an optionally higher premium), it is usually for a limited period only, such as 10 or 20 years. Furthermore, it is typically a promise to index daily benefits by a fixed maximum percentage each year without compounding the increases. This amounts to offering less and less protection against inflation, in percentage terms, each year, making inflation-protected benefits decreasingly adequate the earlier in life that one buys them. This method of inflation protection seems downright deceptive of consumers, and it imposes excessive inflation risk on those buyers who minimize adverse selection through early purchase; it should be discouraged by insurance regulators in favor of compounded interest protection, even if the latter is more costly. Insurers should be encouraged to keep policies affordable by promoting longer waiting periods instead. It is far better to leave shorter stays to be paid for out-of-pocket than to let even steady and predictable inflation continue to erode the real value of ostensibly inflation-protected coverage.

Insurers also have been cautious in their coverage of home care, setting maximum daily benefits at about half of the maximums for institutionalized care rather than at the same level as in the Meiners and Trapnell prototype. Skilled care by professionals or custodial care by licensed home health agencies are usually covered, but homemaker services are not. And access to home health benefits is typically restricted to cases of medical necessity or where activities of daily living are limited, just as in the case of nursing home benefits.

Most policies are financed by level premiums, shifting the high cost of care late in life to a schedule of payments that is constant throughout the coverage period. This makes premiums lower the earlier the contract is purchased. Clearly, insurers are concerned also about adverse selection by those waiting beyond age 65 to purchase long-term-care insurance: premiums are typically two to three times as high for those who begin coverage at age 75 as for those who buy at 65. In contrast, Meiners and Trapnell had estimated, based on population average experience, that the ten-year delay would increase premiums by only about three-quarters. And actual premiums for 65-year-olds are themselves generally at least one-third higher than the Meiners and Trapnell projections: the premium for $80/day coverage, with a 30-day waiting period and a four-year maximum length of stay, usually exceeds $1,000/year. Inflation protection usually costs at least an additional $400/year.

Simulations performed with the Brookings-ICF Long-Term Care Financing Model have made it clear how important inflation protection is for an insurance product that is most affordable before age 65 but most likely to be used after age 85. In simulations covering the period 2016–2020, only model policies with inflation protection covered as much as half of nursing home charges for the insured (Rubin et al. 1989). Inflation-protected policies also provided much greater Medicaid spending reductions (about 10%) in the same simulations than conventional policies (Weiner and Rubin 1989). The authors concluded, however, that the potential for both coverage and Medicaid savings were modest. Because of resource limitations and the uninsurability of prior conditions, no more than about 60% of the elderly would be covered under any of the policy prototypes simulated, and no more than about 15% of expenditures would be reimbursed (Rubin et al. 1989).

Because of the extent to which long-term-care insurance is forward-funded by recent enrollees, its reserves accrue substantial interest and dividends. These are taxed as corporate income, under current law, making premiums unnecessarily

high.[8] It makes little sense to allow taxes to be deferred on retirement savings, such as through Individual Retirement Accounts, while at the same time applying a special tax to savings
earmarked for long-term care, simply because a corporation
provides the service. A change in the tax treatment of long-
term-care insurance, giving its reserves the same tax-exempt
status as those for whole-life insurance, would offer potential
subscribers a fairer premium, relative to their actual risk, and
make it easier to expand the market for this insurance. Some of
the lost tax revenues would be recouped, because Medicaid
spend-down cases would be reduced.

Other legislative proposals have focused on directly encouraging the purchase of insurance: long-term-care insurance
premiums could be made tax deductible for employers, as
health insurance premiums now are, as well as for the insured.
Or where funds have already been accumulated subject to deferred taxation, such as in IRAs or vested pensions, they could
be allowed to be withdrawn tax free if applied to the purchase
of long-term-care insurance (Moran and Weingart 1988).

Early purchase is crucial to avoiding adverse selection, but
the purchase of a long-term-care policy adds a substantial new
item to one's budget. Life insurance policies are a natural
source for the necessary funds (Hughes 1986). Beyond retirement, it is no longer necessary to be insured against earnings
losses, and Social Security and many private pensions provide
insurance against the loss of a spouse's retirement income in
the form of survivors' benefits. Life insurance coverage could
be converted to long-term-care coverage at age 65 (or 67, once it
has become the normal age of eligibility for full Social Security
retirement benefits); those who continue working full-time beyond that age could be offered the option to delay conversion
until age 70. Long-term-care insurance is currently available as
a rider, at additional expense, on some life insurance policies;
conversion of life insurance to long-term-care insurance would
make lower premiums possible by instead terminating or phas-
ing out life insurance coverage at the point where its importance wanes.

A life insurance policy convertible to long-term-care insurance would be most attractive to workers with dependents and
with adequate pension survivorship coverage, because such in-

dividuals need substantial life insurance coverage prior to retirement but not afterward. For single workers, and for those with inadequate pension survivorships, other innovative vehicles may be necessary to promote sufficient new saving to finance an expansion of long-term insurance coverage. The two most prominent proposals are for expansions of the Individual Retirement Account (IRA) concept, and of home equity conversions.

Long-Term-Care IRAs. Individual Retirement Accounts (IRAs) are special accounts for retirement savers, providing income-tax deferral and subject to penalties for early withdrawal. An IRA allows a worker without an employer pension plan, or with annual income below $25,000 (for singles; $40,000 for couples), to defer until withdrawal the income taxes on contributions up to $2000 annually. Taxes on accumulating interest are likewise deferred until withdrawal, and the combination of these two deferrals is equivalent to exempting from taxation all interest earned between contribution and withdrawal, if the saver's tax rate is constant throughout the period. For most who use IRAs, it is likely in addition that the ultimate taxes levied will be at a reduced rate, because total income typically falls at retirement. A justification for this revenue loss is its potential to reduce the need for future transfers, through Social Security, to by themselves provide socially adequate retirement incomes.

Until 1987, full tax deferral was available to all workers, regardless of income or pension coverage. But IRAs offer the greatest tax advantage to those in higher tax brackets; reducing taxes on saving by the affluent (who already save the most) and those with pensions does little to reduce the future need for transfers, but does encourage the shifting of existing savings into tax-advantaged IRAs. Accordingly, in the 1986 Tax Reform Act, Congress eliminated the tax deduction on IRA contributions by high earners and those with pension plans, leaving them only the deferral of taxes on subsequent interest.

The preponderance of available evidence indicates that the IRA has done little to promote saving (Gravelle 1991). In fact, because of its design, the IRA may even reduce saving. Most participants contribute the maximum dollar amount allowed (Galper and Byce 1986). For those whose saving would exceed the $2000 ceiling even without an IRA, the tax deduction leaves the after-tax rate of return to marginal increases in saving unchanged, yet increases lifetime wealth. When current income remains unchanged and lifetime wealth increases, saving tends to fall.

The IRA serves as the model for other proposed tax-advantaged accounts designed to encourage other earmarked private saving, such as the Long-Term-Care IRA (LTCIRA). Direct purchase of care, of insurance, or payment of CCRC entrance fees or S/HMO premiums could all be allowable uses of LTCIRA funds. Workers, however, can already use ordinary IRAs to save for long-term care; to introduce specially earmarked Long Term-Care IRAs would have little additional effect unless designed to provide new tax advantages to savers. One possibility is for LTCIRAs to offer additional tax advantages at withdrawal and to treat insurance more favorably than direct purchases of care: for example, legislation introduced in 1987 would have encouraged insurance by requiring income tax on 80% of distributions from LTCIRAS used to buy care directly, but only 50% on distributions used to purchase insurance (Moran and Weingart 1988).

For high earners, however, these additional tax advantages are probably unnecessary: simply allowing deferral of taxes on income contributed to a LTCIRA, now denied high earners with IRAs, would be a substantial incentive to start an account. A simple way to integrate LTCIRAs and IRAs would be to restore the pre-1986 deductibility of contributions by higher-income workers and those with pensions with the requirement that any fully tax-deductible contributions made by those workers be into LTCIRAs, not IRAs.

Allowing LTCIRA deductions for high earners would not conflict with the intent of the 1986 cutback on deductions into ordinary IRAs. Employer pensions and high incomes may suffice without subsidy as sources of retirement support, but they do not guarantee adequate provision for long-term-care expenses. Only higher earners who already put aside at least $2000 annually intended specifically to provide for future long-term care would receive pure tax windfalls; for all others, the deductibility of LTCIRA contributions would increase the after-tax return to marginal increases in saving. A partial tax credit for contributions, as an alternative to tax deductibility, would make both LTCIRAs and IRAs relatively more attractive to low earners, since the tax advantage would then be independent of income. Either way, the increased accumulation of earmarked funds in LTCIRAs could provide a larger market, enabling private insurance companies to increase their offerings and pass scale economies on to subscribers.

Uncertain of the future cost of insurance and long-term care, some savers would accumulate larger accounts than necessary, especially those ultimately needing the least care. This raises the issue of transferability of the funds to one's heirs. Unless LTCIRA funds were bequeathable, the incentive to spend all funds before death would put excessive upward pressure on the demand for care (Fullerton 1982). On the other hand, if bequests were allowed without penalty, the LTCIRA could be abused as a tax-avoidance device. A penalty on bequests, similar to the one that applies to early withdrawals from IRAs, and exempting bequests to spouses, would deter the use of LTCIRA tax deductions to subsidize ordinary intergenerational transfers. And large penalties for withdrawal from LTCIRAs for unauthorized purposes would be appropriate, in order to prevent their use by high earners to finance early retirement.

Home Equity Conversion. The major asset of most elderly Americans is their home: in 1987, 75% of elderly households were homeowner households, and 83% of those households owned their homes free and clear.[9] The value of a house may exceed the amount that its owner intends to bequeath, yet the excess value of the house is difficult to liquidate without a sale, requiring a disruptive move late in life. As a result, wealth which could otherwise be used to finance needed long-term care or insurance may be tied up in excessive home equity. It is possible for owners to gain access to much of a house's value, however, through a Reverse Annuity Mortgage (RAM).

In a RAM, the homeowner essentially sells the house to a financial institution in return for a lifetime annuity, and the institution in turn rents the house back to the seller: the equivalent of rent is reflected in a decrement to the annuity payments. Thus, those with RAMs pay only for housing services needed while they are alive and have access to the equity in their homes to pay other costs of living, including insurance premiums. If and when the house is sold, whether at the death of the homeowner or before, receipts go to the financial institution rather than to the homeowner or that person's estate. Because older persons have the shortest life expectancies, their potential RAM payments tend to be largest; and since the risk of dependency also rises with age, older single homeowners are the population that could be best served by RAMs (Jacobs and Weissert 1987).

Ideally, RAMs would permit homeowners to liquidate the full values of their houses and provide them with lifetime annuities: this would provide the greatest income security. But financial institutions providing RAMs take risks: there is uncertainty that the house will maintain its value over the remaining lifetime of its resident, not only because of real estate market fluctuations but also because the issuance of a RAM reduces a homeowner's financial interest in keeping the house up. For this reason, RAMs are generally limited to 60%–80% of the house's value. And because the annuity provided by a lifetime RAM would be especially attractive to a healthy homeowner expecting an exceptionally long life, there is an adverse selection problem, as a result of which annuities do not provide actuarially fair incomes. Venti and Wise (1991) estimate that lump-sum reverse mortgages, which would avoid adverse selection with respect to longevity, could increase the liquid wealth of most elderly families by a much greater proportion than lifetime RAMs (providing market-average annuity yields) could increase income. In practice, RAMs are in fact generally limited to terms of 5–10 years, making them hybrids between lump-sum payments and lifetime annuities.

Limiting the term of the annuity has apparent immediate benefits to the homeowner in that it increases the monthly payment supportable by a given amount of equity, but it also increases the likelihood of outliving the contract, forcing a change in residence (Hughes 1986). This makes RAMs, as currently designed, relatively unattractive to the newly retired. CCRCs face a complementary marketing problem: admission is most readily granted to the newly retired who are in good health, but most people at this stage of life look forward to a period of self-sufficiency in their own homes.

Partnerships between mortgage lenders and CCRCs could meet both concerns simultaneously by offering a package combining a RAM for the first 10 years of retirement and a guarantee of admission to a CCRC at the completion of the 10-year term, or upon the death or severe disablement of either spouse. The annuity payments made by the RAM would be net of the CCRC entrance fee. The risks to the partnership inherent in the housing and long-term-care components of this package would tend to offset each other. Early disablement, causing early admission and high expenses to the CCRC, would also relieve the partnership of its obligation to provide housing services in the family home, permitting its early sale. Conversely, those enjoying housing services for the full 10-year term of the RAM would make the smallest lifetime demands on CCRC resources.

Under current tax rules, capital gains from a single home sale, at age 55 or older, are allowed to be excluded from income taxation. Meiners (1983) has suggested that long-term-care insurance could be encouraged by requiring that this exclusion be allowed only to the extent that the proceeds are put toward long-term-care insurance. If such a requirement were adopted, it would be sensible to include RAM-CCRC partnerships (and possibly other creative RAM-insurance combinations) among the allowable uses of tax-deductible funds. This would encourage the newly retired who wish for the time being to remain in their homes to convert home equity into long-term-care coverage, and to do so before aging or unforeseen illness might render them uninsurable.

6

What Can Be Done

WELL BEFORE THE year 2010, when those born in 1945 reach the current age of Medicare eligibility, substantial changes will have to be made in the delivery and financing of medical and long-term care for the aged. Our current system, largely dependent as it is on intergenerational transfers, will soon face growing demands for care, relative to its transfer base. If we passively maintain that system, citizens will have to make difficult choices between continuing improvements in medical and long-term care for the aged versus improvements in the standard of living of workers and their families. Put more narrowly but also concretely, the projected financing difficulties posed by Medicare, Medicaid, and other transfer programs can only be solved by either increasing transfers per worker or by decreasing transfers per aged citizen.

Pay-as-you-go social insurance has made medical care available to a greatly expanded proportion of the elderly since the mid-1960s. If that system is to continue to meet its medical care commitments, as currently defined, then substantial increases in transfers will be necessary, whether or not we increase coverage to fill the most prominent gaps. Possibilities for sufficiently large increases in transfers include

- increasing income and payroll taxes to pay for current programs, and
- creating new pay-as-you-go social insurance programs to cover catastrophic medical and/or long-term-care costs.

Other carefully targeted increases in transfers, although not by themselves sufficient to meet rising demands for medical and long-term-care assistance, could help to dampen the need for care itself. These include

- • increasing excise taxes on cigarettes and alcohol; and
- • requiring families of those receiving government-financed long-term care to meet a deductible, optionally payable in caretaking time.

The first of these would reduce the need for future care, and the second would reduce inefficient overinstitutionalization.

But the demographics of the twenty-first century promise to make transfers to one's elders a poor investment for younger workers. To respond to this concern, shortfalls could instead be met by reducing transfers, per recipient, to the aged. While the relative poverty of the aged would have made cuts in intergenerational transfers unthinkable as recently as 20 years ago, their economic status has improved very substantially in the intervening time.

Some would take this approach to an extreme, arguing that the fairest way to hold the growth of intergenerational transfers in check, as the demand for care grows relative to its base of transfers, is the arbitrary rationing of care by age. This would resolve the trade-off between young and old at the expense of the oldest old, completely insulating other age groups from sacrifice. More broadly based reductions in transfers would permit all of the aged equal access to some measure of covered care, arguably a more just outcome, while still making concessions to the legitimate interests of hard-pressed workers and their families.

Net transfers could be significantly reduced by either of the following broadly based measures:

- • increasing SMI premiums; or
- • imposing an income tax surcharge upon the aged, to be paid into the HI Trust Fund.

But there are additional reductions in transfers that would also be likely to either increase employment by encouraging later retirement, or to counteract the overuse of services due to moral hazard. These include:

- • further delaying the age of eligibility for full Social Security retirement benefits;

- charging a premium for HI eligibility between age 65 and the age of full Social Security eligibility;
- increasing the SMI deductible;
- increasing the SMI coinsurance rate at low levels of annual expense;
- taxing medigap premiums, or requiring medigap policies to meet higher Medicare copayments than are charged to out-of-pocket payers;
- extending prospective payment to a wider range of Medicare- and Medicaid-covered services;
- expanding the prescreening of Medicaid admissions, offering community-based services as an alternative to institutionalized care; and
- converting the financing of state Medicaid programs to a system of block grants.

While some of the changes outlined above could make the medical and long-term-care delivery systems function more efficiently, none would really promote significant overall economic growth, and so none of them can really promise much more than an orderly resolution of conflict between young and old. A better outcome is possible, however: if demographic considerations force us to consider a scaling-down of intergenerational transfers, they also offer saving as the more advantageous way to transfer resources from youth to old age. Saving is the way for Baby Boomers and succeeding generations to offset cuts in transfers and guarantee decent care for themselves after retirement, by investing in the growth of the economy.

Government, in its role as insurer, could promote saving for future care by

- truly prefunding new or existing social insurance programs, reducing government debt to the private sector as trust funds accumulate; and
- permitting Medicare enrollees to elect Social/Health Maintenance Organization enrollment as an alternative to ordinary coverage, financed by Medicare and a supplementary premium.

It could also encourage the substitution of private long-term-care insurance for public assistance by

- relaxing Medicaid income and asset spend-down limits for those who use private insurance to cover some minimum length of stay, and

—• reinstating Medicaid's penalty for recent intrafamily transfers.

Government could, in fact, require private long-term-care coverage for all, providing assistance to those without the means to pay for it. But even without imposing such a requirement, government has considerable power, as taxing authority and insurance regulator, to encourage wider purchase of private long-term-care insurance by such means as

—• liberalizing the tax-deductibility of employer contributions to prefunded retirement health insurance;
—• exempting insurance fund income from corporate taxation;
—• requiring insurers to offer better optional inflation protection, encouraging them to offset the cost with longer waiting periods;
—• restricting capital gains exclusions on home sales to the portion of proceeds used to buy insurance; and
—• permitting those at all income levels to defer income tax on contributions to accounts earmarked for long-term care.

Finally, insurers and financial institutions can promote the expansion of long-term-care insurance by promoting complementary combinations of coverages and other financial arrangements, such as

—• life insurance policies written to convert to long-term-care insurance at retirement;
—• Reverse Annuity Mortgages packaged with prepaid reserved entrance into Continuing Care Retirement Communities; and
—• "long-life" insurance, annuities paired with long-term-care insurance.

When public spending threatens to exceed its resources, it is natural to first focus attention on the finances of the public programs in peril; finding ways to increase revenues here and to reduce benefits there in order to achieve budgetary balance is usually the simplest way to avoid a shortfall. Indeed, when social insurance trust funds face imminent exhaustion, the need to continue timely benefit payments makes quick and easily understood fine-tuning adjustments necessary. But we face no such short-term crisis: time remains to provide thoughtfully and plentifully for the twenty-first century that we foresee, if we begin soon.

In contrast to simple modifications of existing programs, the creation and marketing of innovative insurance products is likely to be a challenging and sometimes discouraging trial-and-error process, but its promise is also much greater. Indeed, it is our best hope for making a healthy, secure, and decent retirement possible for all, after Baby Boomers reach the ends of their working lives.

NOTES

Chapter One

1. See Board of Trustees, Federal Hospital Insurance Trust Fund (1991); Board of Trustees, Federal Old Age and Survivors Insurance and Disability Insurance Trust Funds (1991); Rice and Feldman (1983); and Spencer (1989). Rates of change of nursing home residency, disability, and hospitalization are expressed relative to 1990 for expositional reasons, where 1990 base figures are estimated by averaging data and projections from Rice and Feldman (1983), for years 1980 and 2000, respectively.

2. See Spencer (1989), table 4.

3. Ibid., table 1.

4. Ibid., tables G and B5; and U.S. Public Health Service (1988), table 6-3.

5. Personal saving remains between 4% and 5% of personal disposable income, well below the usual post–World War II range of 7%–9%. See Council of Economic Advisors (1991a), table B26.

Chapter Two

1. See U.S. Bureau of the Census (1989), table 743.

2. See Social Security Administration (1991), table 3E2.

3. Ibid., table 3D1.

4. See U.S. Bureau of the Census (1991), table 22.

5. Ibid. (1990), table 108.

6. Ibid. (1991), table 106.

7. The duration of chronic illness may decrease as an absolute amount, or as a fraction of the lifetime. Fries (1983) calls these absolute and relative compression of morbidity. The former tends to reduce the absolute size of the chronically ill population, while the latter tends to reduce the fraction of the population that is chronically ill.

8. They note that Manitoban nursing homes include some lighter-care residents who in the United States might instead be in residential care, but do not include shorter rehabilitative stays, so that the Manitobans tend to enter nursing homes later and stay longer than U.S. residents.

9. See U.S. Bureau of the Census (1991), table 107.

10. For example, GNP takes no account of nonmarket goods or bads, and includes production of capital goods, which promote only future well-being, along with consumption goods, which can be enjoyed immediately.

11. This calculation assumes a five-year reduction in a 1990 baseline career beginning at age 20 and ending at age 62. The resulting average annual rate of decline in career length is about −.25% when spread over a 50-year period.

12. See Council of Economic Advisors (1990), pp. 40–41.

13. In addition to utilization, Rice and Feldman also projected expenditures. The age categories they used for the latter projections were overly broad, however, so that by assuming fixed age-specific rates they failed to allow for aging within the aged population. The HCFA (1987) projections also attempted to account for the effect of demographic changes on the intensity of care per incident of use. The only effects were very small changes in growth rates of hospital utilization.

Chapter Three

1. Myers (1985, pp. 480–481) estimates, for example, that a male worker aged 65 in 1984 and earning 50% of maximum covered earnings since 1937 would receive OASDI benefits equal to 2.79 times the accumulated value (with interest) of his employee OASDI payroll taxes.

2. In fact, increased savings in neoclassical models of economic growth increase per capita consumption if and only if r exceeds $(w + n)$. See Solow (1970).

3. See U.S. Bureau of the Census (1991), table 632.

4. Ibid., tables 13 and 145.

5. See Social Security Administration (1991), tables 7.B.1 and 7.B.2.

6. Ibid., table 7.B.10.

7. Ibid., table 7.A.1.

8. See Board of Trustees, Federal Supplementary Medical Insurance Trust Fund (1991), table 1.

9. See U.S. Bureau of the Census (1990), table 150; and Social Security Administration (1991), table 2.A.14.

10. See Board of Trustees, Federal Old Age and Survivors Insurance and Disability Insurance Trust Funds (1991), table G1.

11. See U.S. Bureau of the Census (1990), tables 150 and 757.

12. See Board of Trustees, Federal Hospital Insurance Trust Fund (1991), table A1.

13. There is an important difference: after the awarding of an individual's initial Social Security retirement benefit, his or her benefit increases only in proportion to consumer price inflation. Only initial benefits awarded to successive birth cohorts of new retirees rise at the generally higher rate of wage inflation.

14. See Board of Trustees, Federal Old Age and Survivors Insurance and Disability Insurance Trust Funds (1991), table A1, and pp. 101–102.

15. See Board of Trustees, Federal Hospital Insurance Trust Fund (1991), p. 47.

16. See Board of Trustees, Federal Old Age and Survivors Insurance and Disability Insurance Trust Funds (1991), table 11.

17 See Board of Trustees, Federal Hospital Insurance Trust Fund (1991), table 10.

18. Ibid., table 6; and Board of Trustees, Federal Supplementary Medical Insurance Trust Fund (1991), table 6.

19. See Board of Trustees, Federal Hospital Insurance Trust Fund (1991), table 9. SMI costs are assumed in these calculations to remain at 66% of HI costs.

20. This is the difference between OASDI's 13.11% projected income rate under intermeduate assumptions, over the period 1991–2065, and its combined payroll tax rate of 12.40%. See Board of Trustees, Federal Old Age and Survivors Insurance and Disability Trust Funds (1991), tables 27 and 29.

21. See Board of Trustees, Federal Old Age and Survivors Insurance and Disability Insurance Trust Funds (1991), table 27.

22. See U.S. Public Health Service (1988), vol. 2, sec. 6, table 6-3.

23. See Social Security Administration (1991), tables 4.B1 and 7.A1.

24. Ibid., table 7.E2.

25. Ibid., table 7.E1.

26. See U.S. Office of Management and Budget (1990).

27. See Social Security Administration (1991), table 7.E2.

28. Ibid., tables 7.A1, 7.A2, and 7.E2.

29. Ibid., table 7.E1.

Chapter Four

1. See US Bureau of the Census (1991), table 154.

2. Rothschild and Stiglitz originally argued that the market depicted in figure 4.2 would not have a stable equilibrium, but instability disappears if firms refrain from offering contracts that would ultimately result in losses (Cave 1985).

3. Note that an indifference curve through α^L (h_α in figure 1) would lie below and to the left of h_β. This only occurs if the line $\alpha^L\beta^L$ is steep relative to the indifference curve h_α, which is why the subsidy equilibrium in figure 2 requires a certain proportion of the population to be low risks, making the subsidy per low-risk policyholder sufficiently small.

4. Intermediate possibilities would be combinations of policies from $\beta^H\gamma$ and $\beta^L\gamma$, respectively, each pair sharing a high-risk indifference curve.

5. Eichenbaum and Peled (1987) have shown that imposition of a mandatory fair pooled annuity can increase incomes of both high and low risks where there is adverse selection. This is an important argument for imposing an actuarially fair pooled social security system where there is none.

6. See Social Security Administration (1991), tables 4.A.2, 7.A.1, and 7.A.2.

7. Wolfe and Goddeeris (1991), however, demonstrate that some of the apparent moral hazard effect of medigap coverage on spending may be attributable to adverse selection.

8. See U.S. Bureau of the Census (1991), table 154.

Chapter Five

1. See Board of Trustees, Federal Supplementary Medical Insurance Trust Fund (1991), table 5.

2. SMI bills are classified into either surgical or medical, depending on the highest-priced service included in the bill. See Social Security Administration, (June 1991), table Q-15.

3. See Social Security Administration (1991), table 2.A.14.

4. See U.S. Bureau of the Census (1991), tables 148 and 471.

5. See sources cited in ibid.

6. Much of the information in the next four paragraphs about currently available policies comes from this excellent report.

7. Meiners (1983) reports that 45% of stays are less than 90 days in length. Liu and Manton (1983) found that 64% of 1976 admissions had stays of less than 90 days in 1976, some of those stays having been truncated by the end of the calendar year.

8. Meiners and Trapnell (1984) estimated that corporate income taxes accounted for 21% of their estimated premium, but the 1986 Tax Reform Act has subsequently reduced corporate income tax rates, so that potential premium reductions from a lifting of the tax would now be less than 21%.

9. See U.S. Bureau of the Census (1990), tables 1277 and 1278.

REFERENCES

Aaron, Henry. 1966. "The Social Insurance Paradox." *Canadian Journal of Economics and Political Science* 32, no. 3 (August).

Aaron, Henry J., and Schwartz, William B. 1984. *The Painful Prescription: Rationing Hospital Care.* Washington, D.C.: Brookings Institution.

Atkins, G. Lawrence. 1985. "The Economic Status of the Oldest Old." *Milbank Memorial Fund Quarterly/Health and Society* 63, no. 2:395–419.

Battin, Margaret P. 1987. "Age Rationing and the Just Distribution of Health Care: Is There a Duty to Die?" In *Should Medical Care be Rationed by Age?* ed. Timothy Smeeding. Totowa, NJ: Rowman and Littlefield.

Bishop, Christine. 1981. "A Compulsory National Long-Term Care Insurance Program." In *Reforming the Long-Term Care System,* ed. James J. Callahan, Jr., and Stanley Wallack. Lexington, MA: Lexington Books.

Board of Trustees, Federal Hospital Insurance Trust Fund. 1991. *Annual Report.* Washington, D.C.: Government Printing Office.

Board of Trustees, Federal Old Age and Survivors Insurance and Disability Insurance Trust Funds. 1991. *Annual Report.* Washington, D.C.: Government Printing Office.

Board of Trustees, Federal Supplementary Medical Insurance Trust Fund. 1991. *Annual Report.* Washington, D.C.: Government Printing Office.

Boskin, M. J. 1986. *Too Many Promises: The Uncertain Future of Social Security.* New York: Dow Jones-Irwin.

Boskin, M. J.; Avrin, M.; and Cone, K. 1983. "Modelling Alternative Solutions to the Long-Run Social Security Funding Problem." In *Behavioral Simulation Models in Tax Analysis,* ed. M. S. Feldstein. Chicago, IL: University of Chicago Press.

Boskin, M. J.; Kotlikoff, L. J.; Puffert, D. J.; and Shoven, J. B. 1987. "Social Security: A Financial Appraisal across and within Generations." *National Tax Journal* 40, no. 1 (March): 19–34.

Brecher, C., and Knickman, J. 1985. "A Reconsideration of Long-Term Health Policy." *Journal of Health Politics, Policy, and Law* 10:245–272.

Brody, Jacob A., and Schneider, Edward L. 1986. "Diseases and Disorders of Aging: An Hypothesis." *Journal of Chronic Disability* 39, no. 11:871–876.

Buchanan, Robert J. 1983. "Medicaid Cost Containment: Prospective Reimbursement for Long-Term Care." *Inquiry* 20 (Winter): 334–342.

Bureau of Old Age and Survivors Insurance. 1959. "Resources and Health Status of OASI Beneficiaries." *Monthly Labor Review* 82 (August): 882.

Callahan, D. 1987. *Setting Limits: Medical Goals in an Aging Society.* New York: Simon and Schuster.

Callahan, James, et al. 1980. "Responsibility of Families for Their Severely Disabled Elders." *Health Care Financing Review* 1 (Winter): 29–48.

Cave, Jonathan A. K. 1985. "Subsidy Equilibrium and Multiple Option Insurance Markets." *Advances in Health Economics and Health Services Research* 16:27–45.

Chiswick, Barry. 1976. "The Demand for Nursing Home Care: An Analysis of the Substitution between Institutional and Noninstitutional Care." *Journal of Human Resources* (Summer).

Cohen, Marc A. 1988. "Life Care: New Options for Financing and Delivering Long-Term Care." *Health Care Financing Review.* Annual Supplement: 139–143.

Cohen, Marc A.; Tell, Eileen J.; Greenberg, Jay N.; and Wallack, Stanley S. 1987. "The Financial Capacity of the Elderly to

Insure for Long-Term Care." *The Gerontologist* 27, no. 4:494–502.

Congressional Budget Office. 1990. *Federal Taxation of Tobacco, Alcoholic Beverages, and Motor Fuels.* Washington, D.C.: Government Printing Office.

Consumers Union. 1991. "An Empty Promise to the Elderly?" *Consumer Reports* 56, no. 6 (June): 425–442.

Cooper, Russell. 1984. "On Allocative Distortions in Problems of Self-Selection." *Rand Journal of Economics* 15, no. 4 (Winter): 568–577.

Council of Economic Advisors. 1990. *Economic Report of the President.* Washington, D.C.: Government Printing Office.

———. 1991a. *Economic Report of the President.* Washington, D.C.: Government Printing Office.

———. 1991b. *Economic Indicators* (April). Washington, D.C.: Government Printing Office.

Cresta, Jean-Paul, and Laffont, Jean-Jacques. 1987. "Incentive Compatibility of Insurance and the Value of Information." *Journal of Risk and Insurance* 54, no. 3:520–540.

Daniels, N. 1983. "Justice between Age Groups: Am I My Parents' Keeper?" *Milbank Memorial Fund Quarterly/Health and Society* 61:489–522.

———. 1988. *Am I My Parents' Keeper: An Essay on Justice between the Young and the Old.* New York: Oxford University Press.

Davis, Karen, and Rowland, Diane. 1986. *Medicare Policy: New Directions for Health and Long-Term Care.* Baltimore and London: Johns Hopkins University Press.

DesHarnais, Susan; Kobrinski, Edward; Chesney, James; Long, Michael; Ament, Richard; and Fleming, Steven. 1987. "The Early Effects of the Prospective Payment System on Inpatient Utilization and the Quality of Care." *Inquiry* 24 (Spring): 7–16.

Diamond, Larry M., and Berman, David E. 1981. "The Social/Health Maintenance Organization: A Single Entry, Prepaid, Long-Term-Care-Delivery System." In *Reforming the Long-Term Care System,* ed. James Callahan and Stanley Wallack. Lexington, MA: D. C. Heath and Co.

Doty, Pamela. 1986. "Family Care of the Elderly: The Role of Public Policy." *Health and Society/The Milbank Quarterly* 64, no. 1:34–75.

Dowd, Bryan, and Feldman, Roger. 1985. "Biased Selection in Twin Cities Health Plans." *Advances in Health Economics and Health Services Research* 6:253–271.

Eggers, P. 1980. "Risk Differential between Medicare Beneficiaries Enrolled and Not Enrolled in an HMO." *Health Care Financing Review* 1:91–99.

Eggers, P., and Prihoda, H. 1982. "Pre-enrollment Reimbursement Patterns of Medicare Beneficiaries Enrolled in At-Risk HMOs." *Health Care Financing Review* 4:55–74.

Eichenbaum, Martin S., and Peled, Dan. 1987. "Capital Accumulation and Annuities in an Adverse Selection Economy." *Journal of Political Economy* 95, no. 2:334–354.

Ellis, Randall P., and McGuire, Thomas G. 1986. "Provider Behavior under Prospective Reimbursement." *Journal of Health Economics* 5:129–151.

Enthoven, Alain. 1987. "The Health Care Economy in the U.S.A." In *Health Economics: Prospects for the Future,* ed. George Teeling Smith. Beckenham, Kent: Croom Helm Ltd.

Farley, Pamela J., and Monheit, Alan C. 1985. "Selectivity in the Demand for Health Insurance and Health Care." *Advances in Health Economics and Health Services Research* 6: 231–248.

Feldman, Jacob J. 1983. "Work Ability of the Aged under Conditions of Improving Mortality." *Milbank Memorial Fund Quarterly/Health and Society* 61, no. 3:430–444.

Feldstein, Martin. 1971. "A New Approach to National Health Insurance." *Public Interest* 23:93–105.

Feldstein, Paul J. 1988. *Health Care Economics.* New York: John Wiley and Sons.

Frech, H. E. III. 1985. "The Property Rights Theory of the Firm: Some Evidence from the U.S. Nursing Home Industry." *Zeitschrift für die Gesamte Staatswissenschaft/ Journal of Institutional and Theoretical Economics* 141, no. 1:146–166.

Frech, H. E. III, and Ginsberg, Paul B. 1987. *Public Insurance in Private Medical Markets.* Washington, D.C.: American Enterprise Institute.

Freeman, Richard. 1986. "The Demand for Education." Pp. 357–386 in *The Handbook of Labor Economics*, ed. O Ashenfelter and R. Layard. Vol. 1. Amsterdam: Elsevier Science Publishers.

Fries, James F. 1980. "Aging, Natural Death, and the Compression of Morbidity." *New England Journal of Medicine* 303, no. 3:130–135.

———. 1983. "The Compression of Morbidity." *Milbank Memorial Fund Quarterly/Health and Society* 61, no. 3:397–419.

———. 1984. "The Compression of Morbidity: Miscellaneous Comments about a Theme." *The Gerontologist* 24, no. 4:354–359.

———. 1989. "The Compression of Morbidity: Near or Far?" *Milbank Memorial Fund Quarterly/Health and Society* 67, no. 2:208–232.

Fries, James F., and Crapo, L. M. 1981. *Vitality and Aging.* San Francisco: W. H. Freeman.

Fuchs, Victor. 1984. "Though Much Is Taken: Reflections on Aging, Health, and Medical Care." *Milbank Memorial Fund Quarterly/Health and Society* 62:143–166.

Fullerton, William D. 1982. "Finding the Money and Paying for Long-Term Care Services: The Devil's Briarpatch." Pp. 182–208 in *Policy Options in Long-Term Care,* ed. Judith Meltzer, Frank Farrow, and Harold Richmond, Chicago: University of Chicago Press.

Galper, Harvey, and Byce, Charles. 1986. "Individual Retirement Accounts: Facts and Issues." *Tax Notes* (June 2):917–921.

Getzen, Thomas E. 1988. "Long-Life Insurance: A Prototype for Funding Long-Term Care." *Health Care Financing Review* 10, no. 2 (Winter): 47–56.

Gravelle, Jane G. 1991. "Do Individual Retirement Accounts Increase Savings?" *Journal of Economic Perspectives* 5, no. 2 (Spring): 133–148.

Greenberg, Jay N., Leutz, Walter N.; and Abrahams, Ruby. 1985. "The National Social Health Maintenance Organization Demonstration." *Journal of Ambulatory Care Management* 8, no. 4:32–61.

Greenberg, Jay N.; Leutz, Walter N.; Greenlick, Merwyn; Malone, Joelyn; Ervin, Sam; and Kodner, Dennis. 1988. "The Social HMO Demonstration: Early Experience." *Health Affairs* 7, no. 3 (Summer): 66–79.

Gruenberg, Ernest M. 1977. "The Failure of Success." *Milbank Memorial Fund Quarterly*/Health and Society 55, no. 3 (Summer): 3–24.

Guralnik, Jack M.; Yanagishita, Machiko; and Schneider, Edward L. 1988. "Projecting the Older Population of the United States: Lessons from the Past and Prospects for the Future." *Milbank Memorial Fund Quarterly/Health and Society* 66, no. 2:283–308.

Guterman, Stuart; Eggers, Paul; Riley, Gerald; Green, Timothy F.; and Terrell, Sherry A. 1988. "The First 3 Years of Medicare Prospective Payment: An Overview." *Health Care Financing Review* 9, no. 3 (Spring): 67–77.

Harrington, Charlene, and Swan, James. 1984. "Medicaid Nursing Home Reimbursement Policies, Rates, and Expenditures." *Health Care Financing Review* 6, no. 1 (Fall).

Health Care Financing Administration, Office of the Actuary, Division of National Cost Estimates. 1987. *Health Care Financing Review* 8, no. 4 (Summer): 1–36.

Horowitz, Amy, and Shindelman, Lois W. 1983. "Social and Economic Incentives for Family Caregivers," *Health Care Financing Review* 5, no. 2:25–33.

Hughes, Susan L. 1986. *Long-Term Care: Options in an Expanding Market.* Homewood, IL.: Dow Jones-Irwin.

Hughes, Susan L.; Cordray, David; and Spiker, V. Alan. 1984. "Evaluation of Long-Term Home Care Program." *Medical Care* (May): 460.

Hurd, Michael D. 1990. "Research on the Elderly: Economic Status, Retirement, and Consumption and Saving." *Journal of Economic Literature* 28, no. 2 (June): 565–637.

Jackson-Beeck, Marilyn, and Kleinman, John H. 1983. "Evidence for Self-Selection among Health Maintenance Organization Enrolles." *JAMA* 250, no. 20 (November 25):2826–2829.

Jacobs, Bruce, and Weissert, William. 1987. "Using Home Equity to Finance Long-Term Care." *Journal of Health Politics, Policy and Law* 12, no. 1 (Spring): 77–95.

Klein, Daniel L., and Petertil, Jeffrey P. 1986. "Health Coverage for Retirees: A Time Bomb." *Personnel* (August): 54–62.

Kohn, R. R. 1982. "Causes of Death in Very Old People." *Journal of the American Medical Association* 247:2793–2979.

Kovar, Mary Grace. 1986. "Expenditures for the Medical Care of Elderly People Living in the Community in 1980." *Health and Society/The Milbank Quarterly* 64, no. 1:100–132.

Kramer, Morton. 1980. "The Rising Pandemic of Mental Disorders and Associated Chronic Diseases and Disabilities." In *Epidemiological Research and a Basis for Organization of Extramural Psychiatry*, ed. E. Strömgen, A. Dupont, and J. A. Nielsen. (Proceedings of the Second European Symposium on Social Psychiatry, Psychiatric Hospital, Aarhus, September 9–28, 1979, Munskgaard, Copenhagen). (Supplement 285), 62:382–397.

Lamm, R. D. 1984. Long Time Dying. *New Republic* 191, no. 9 (August 27): 20–23.

Leutz, Walter. 1986. "Long-Term Care for the Elderly: Public Dreams and Private Realities." *Inquiry* 23 (Summer): 134–140.

Leutz, Walter, and Greenberg, Jay N. 1985. "The Future Financing of Long-Term Care for Older Persons." In *Aging 2000: Our Health Care Destiny*, ed. Charles M. Gaitz et al. Vol. 2. New York: Springer-Verlag.

Liu, Korbin, and Manton, Kenneth G. 1983. "The Characteristics and Utilization Pattern of an Admission Cohort of Nursing Home Patients." *The Gerontologist* 23, no. 1:92–98.

Liu, Korbin; Manton, Kenneth G.; and Allison, Wiley S. 1982. "Demographic and Epidemiological Determinants of Expenditures." Pp. 81–102 in *Long Term Care: Perspectives from Research and Demonstrations*, ed. Ronald J. Vogel and Hans C. Palmer. Baltimore: HCFA.

Long, S. H., and Smeeding, T. M. 1984. "Alternative Medicare Financing Sources." *Milbank Memorial Fund Quarterly/Health and Society* 62, no. 2:325–348.

Lubitz, James, and Prihoda, Ronald. 1984. "The Use and Costs of Medicare Services in the Last 2 Years of Life." *Health Care Financing Review* 5, no. 3 (Spring): 117–131.

Luft, Harold S. 1984. "On the Use of Vouchers for Medicare." *Milbank Memorial Fund Quarterly/Health and Society* 62, no. 2:237–250.

Manning, Willard G.; Newhouse, Joseph P., Duan, Naihua; Keeler, Emmett B.; Leibowitz, Arleen; and Marquis, M. Susan. 1987. "Health Insurance and the Demand for Medical Care: Evidence from a Randomized Experiment." *American Economic Review* 77, no. 3:251–277.

Manton, Kenneth G. 1982. "Changing Concepts of Morbidity and Mortality in the Elderly Population." *Milbank Memorial Fund Quarterly/Health and Society* 60, no. 2:183–244.

———. 1986a. "Cause-Specific Mortality Patterns among the Oldest Old: Multiple Cause of Death Trends, 1968 to 1980." *Journal of Gerontology* 41, no. 2:282–289.

———. 1986b. "Past and Future Life Expectancy Increases at Later Ages: Their Implications for the Linkage of Chronic Morbidity, Disability, and Mortality." *Journal of Gerontology* 41, no. 5:672–681.

Manton, Kenneth G., and Liu, Korbin. 1984. "Projecting Chronic Disease Prevalence." *Medical Care* 22, no. 6:511–526.

Manton, Kenneth G., and Soldo, Beth J. 1985. "Dynamics of Health Changes in the Oldest Old: New Perspectives and Evidence." *Milbank Memorial Fund Quarterly/Health and Society* 63, no. 2:206–285.

Marquis, M. Susan, and Phelps, Charles E. 1987. "Price Elasticity and Adverse Selection in the Demand for Supplementary Health Insurance." *Economic Inquiry* 25, no. 2 (April): 299–313.

Meiners, Mark R. 1983. "The Case for Long-Term Care Insurance," *Health Affairs* 2 (Summer): 55–79.

———. 1988. "Reforming Long-Term Care Financing through Insurance." *Health Care Financing Review.* Supplement: 109–112.

Meiners, Mark R., and Trapnell, Gordon R. 1984. "Long-term Care Insurance: Premium Estimates for Prototype Policies." *Medical Care* 22, no. 10 (October): 901–907.

Minaker, Kenneth L., and Rowe, John. 1985. "Health and Disease among the Oldest Old." *Milbank Memorial Fund Quarterly/Health and Society* 63, no. 2: 324–349.

Miyazaki, H. 1977. "The Rat Race and Internal Labor Markets." *Bell Journal of Economics* (Autumn).

Moon, Marilyn. 1983. "The Role of the Family in the Economic Well-Being of the Elderly." *The Gerontologist* 23, no. 1: 45–50.

Moran, Donald W., and Weingart, Janet M. 1988. "Long-Term Care Financing through Federal Tax Incentives." *Health Care Financing Review.* Supplement: 117–121.

Murray, Charles. 1984. *Losing Ground: American Social Policy, 1950–1980.* New York: Basic Books.

Myers, Daniel A.; Burkhauser, Richard V.; and Holden, Karen C. 1987. "The Transition from Wife to Widow: The Importance of Survivor Benefits to Widows." *Journal of Risk and Insurance* 54 (December): 752–759.

Myers, George C., and Manton, Kenneth G. 1984. "Compression of Mortality: Myth or Reality." *The Gerontologist* 24, no. 4: 346–353.

Myers, Robert J. 1985. *Social Security.* 3d ed. Homewood, IL: Richard D. Irwin, Inc.

National Academy of Social Insurance, 1990. "Congress Returns to Find Social Security Tax Cut a Major Topic." *Social Insurance Update* 11 (February): 1.

National Commission on Social Security Reform. 1983. *Report.* Washington, D.C.: Government Printing Office.

Neipp, Joachim, and Zeckhauser, Richard. 1985. *Advances in Health Economics and Health Services Research* 6:47–72.

Newhouse, Joseph P., and Byrne, Daniel J. 1988. "Did Medicare's Prospective Payment System Cause Length of Stay to Fall?" *Journal of Health Economics* 7:413–416.

Office of the Actuary, Health Care Financing Administration. 1987. "National Health Expenditures, 1986–2000." *Health Care Financing Review* 8, no. 4 (Summer): 1–36.

Olshansky, S. Jay. 1985. "Pursuing Longevity: Delay vs. Elimination of Degenerative Diseases." *American Journal of Public Health* 75, no. 7: 754–757.

———. 1988. "On Forecasting Mortality." *Health and Society/ The Milbank Memorial Fund Quarterly* 66, no. 3: 482–530.

Palmer, John. 1988. "Financing Health Care and Retirement for the Aged." In *Challenge to Leadership,* ed. J. Sawhill. Washington, D.C.: Urban Institute Press.

Palmore, Erdman B. 1986. "Trends in the Health of the Aged." *The Gerontologist* 26, no. 3: 298–302.

Paringer, Lynn. 1983. "Economic Incentives in the Provision of Long-Term Care." In *Market Reforms in Health Care,* ed. Jack Meyer. Washington, D.C.: American Enterprise Institute.

Pauly, Mark V. 1985. "What Is Adverse about Adverse Selection?" *Advances in Health Economics and Health Services Research* 6:281–286.

———. 1986. "Taxation, Health Insurance, and Market Failure in the Medical Economy." *Journal of Economic Literature* 25, no. 2:629–675.

———. 1990. "The Rational Nonpurchase of Long-Term-Care Insurance." *Journal of Political Economy* 98, no. 1 (February): 153–168.

Pellechio, A. J., and Goodfellow, G. P. 1983. "Individual Gains and Losses from Social Security before and after the 1983 Amendments." *Cata Journal* (Fall).

Price, James R., and Mays, James W. 1985. "Selection and the Competitive Standing of Health Plans in a Multiple-Choice, Multiple Insurer Market." *Advances in Health Economics and Health Services Research* 6:127–147.

Ramsey, Frank. 1927. "A Contribution to the Theory of Taxation." *Economic Journal* 37:47–61.

Rice, Dorothy P., and Feldman, Jacob J. 1983. "Living Longer in the United States: Demographic Changes and Health Needs of the Elderly." *Milbank Memorial Fund Quarterly/ Health and Society* 61, no. 3: 384.

Rice, Thomas. 1987. "An Economic Assessment of Health Care Coverage for the Elderly." *Milbank Memorial Fund Quarterly/Health and Society* 65, no. 4: 488–520.

Rice, Thomas, and McCall, Nelda. 1985. "The Extent of Ownership and Characteristics of Medicare Supplemental Policies." *Inquiry* 22 (Summer): 188–200.

Riley, M. W., and Bond, K. 1983. "Beyond Ageism: Postponing the Onset of Disability." Pp. 243–252 in *Aging in Society: Selected Reviews of Recent Research,* ed. M. W. Riley, B. B. Hess, and K. Bond. Hillsdale, NJ: Lawrence Erlbaum Associates.

Roemer, Milton I., et al. 1975. "Copayments for Ambulatory Care: Penny-Wise and Pound-Foolish." *Medical Care* 13:457–466.

Roos, Noralou P.; Montgomery, Patrick; and Roos, Leslie L. 1987. "Health Care Utilization in the Years Prior to Death." *Health and Society* 65, no. 2:231–254.

Rosenwaike, Ira. 1985. "A Demographic Portrait of the Oldest Old." *Milbank Memorial Fund Quarterly/Health and Society* 63, no. 2:187–205.

Rothschild, Michael, and Stiglitz, Joseph. 1976. "Equilibrium in Competitive Insurance Markets: An Essay on the Economics of Imperfect Information." *Quarterly Journal of Economics* 60, no. 4 (November): 629–649.

Rubin, Rose M.; Weiner, Joshua M.; and Meiners, Mark R. 1989. "Private Long-Term Care Insurance: Simulations of a Potential Market." *Medical Care* 27, no. 2 (February): 182–193.

Ruchlin, Hirsch S. 1988. "Continuing Care Retirement Communities: An Analysis of Financial Viability and Health Care Coverage." *The Gerontologist* 28, no. 2:156–162.

Ruchlin, Hirsch; Morris, John; and Eggert, Gerald. 1982. "Management and Financing of Long-Term Care Services—a New Approach to a Chronic Problem." *New England Journal of Medicine* 306 (January 14): 101–105.

Sammartino, Frank J. 1987. "The Effect of Health on Retirement." *Social Security Bulletin* 50, no. 2:31–48.

Samuelson, Paul. 1958. "An Exact Consumption-Loan Model of Interest with or without the Social Contrivance of Money." *Journal of Political Economy* 66 (December): 467–482.

Scanlon, William J. 1980. "A Theory of the Nursing Home Market." *Inquiry* 17 (Spring): 25–41.

Schneider, Edward L., and Brody, Jacob A. 1983. "Aging, Natural Death, and the Compression of Morbidity: Another View." *New England Journal of Medicine* 309, no. 14:854–855.

Sloan, Frank A.; Morrisey, Michael A.; and Valvona, Joseph. 1988. "Effects of the Medicare Prospective Payment System on Hospital Cost Containment: An Early Appraisal." *Health and Society* 66, no. 2: 191–220.

Smeeding, Timothy. 1989. "Full Income Estimates of the Relative Well-Being of the Elderly and Nonelderly." In *Research in Income Inequality,* ed. Daniel Slottje and David Bloom. Vol. 1. Amsterdam: JAI Press.

Social Security Administration. 1991. Annual Statistical Supplement, *Social Security Bulletin.* Washington, D.C.: Government Printing Office.

Solow, Robert. 1970. *Growth Theory: An Exposition.* New York: Oxford University Press.

Sorkin, Alan L. 1986. *Health Care and the Changng Economic Environment.* Lexington, MA: D. C. Heath.

Spence, Michael. 1978. "Product Differentiation and Performance in Insurance Markets." *Journal of Public Economics* 10: 427–447.

Spencer, Gregory. 1989. *Projections of the Population of the United States by Age, Sex, and Race: 1988 to 2080.* U.S Bureau of the Census Current Population Reports, series P-25, no. 1018. Washington, D.C.: Government Printing Office.

Stiglitz, Joseph. 1977. "Monopoly, Nonlinear Pricing, and Imperfect Information." *Review of Economic Studies* 44, no. 3: 407–430.

Taylor, Amy K.; Farley, Pamela J.; and Horgan, Constance M. 1988. "Medigap Insurance: Friend or Foe in Reducing Medicare Deficits?" Pp. 145–177 in *Health Care in America: The Political Economy of Hospitals and Health Insurance,* ed. H. E. Frech III. San Francisco: Pacific Research Institute for Public Policy.

Tell, Eileen J.; Cohen, Marc A.; Larsen, Mary Jo; and Batten, Helen L. 1987a. "Assessing the Elderly's Preferences for Lifecare Retirement Options." *The Gerontologist* 27, no. 4: 503–509.

Tell, Eileen J.; Cohen, Marc A.; and Wallack, Stanley S. 1987b. "Life Care at Home: A New Model for Financing and Delivering Long-Term Care." *Inquiry* 24, no. 3 (Fall): 245–252.

Torrey, Barbara Boyle. 1985. "Sharing Increasing Costs on Declining Income: The Visible Dilemma of the Invisible Aged." *Milbank Memorial Fund Quarterly/Health and Society* 63, no. 2: 377–394.

Trustees of the HI and SMI Trust Funds. 1991. "Actuarial Status of the HI and SMI Trust Funds." *Social Security Bulletin* 53:6 (June): 12–25.

U.S. Bureau of the Census. 1989. *Statistical Abstract of the United States.* Washington, D.C.: Government Printing Office.

———. 1990. *Statistical Abstract of the United States.* Washington, D.C.: Government Printing Office.

———. 1991. *Statistical Abstract of the United States.* Washington, D.C.: Government Printing Office.

U.S. Office of Management and Budget. 1990. *Budget of the United States Government, Fiscal Year 1991.* Washington, D.C.: Government Printing Office.

U.S. Public Health Service. 1988 and earlier years. *Vital Statistics of the United States: Life Tables.* Washington, D.C.: Government Printing Office.

Venti, Steven F., and Wise, David A. 1991. "Aging and the Income Value of Housing Wealth." *Journal of Public Economics* 44, no. 3: 371–397.

Verbrugge, Lois M. 1984. "Longer Life But Worsening Health? Trends in Health and Mortality of Middle-Aged and Older Persons." *Milbank Memorial Fund Quarterly/Health and Society* 62, no. 3: 475–519.

Wallack, Stanley S. 1988. "Recent Trends in the Financing of Long-Term Care." *Health Care Financing Review.* Supplement: 97–102.

Warshawsky, Mark. 1988. "Private Annuity Markets in the United States. *Journal of Risk and Insurance* 55, no. 3 (September): 518–528.

———. 1989. "Postretirement Health Benefit Plans: Costs and Liabilities for Private Employers ," Finance and Economics Discussion Series #76, Federal Reserve Board, Washington, D.C.

Weiner, Joshua M.; Ehrenworth, Deborah A.; and Spence, Denise A. 1987. "Private Long-Term Care Insurance: Cost, Coverage, and Restrictions." *The Gerontologist* 27, no. 4: 487–493.

Weiner, Joshua M., and Rubin, Rose M. 1989. "The Potential Impact of Private Long-Term Care Financing Options on

Medicaid: The Next Thirty Years." *Journal of Health Politics, Policy and Law* 14, no. 2 (Summer): 327–340.

Welch, W. P. 1985a. "Health Care Utilization in HMOs: Results from Two National Samples." *Journal of Health Economics* 4: 293–308.

———. 1985b. "Regression toward the Mean in Medical Care Costs." *Medical Care* 23, no. 11: 1234–1241.

Wilson, Catherine E., and Weissert, William G. 1989. "Private Long-Term-Care Insurance: After Coverage Restrictions Is There Anything Left?" *Inquiry* 26, no. 3 (Winter): 493–507.

Wolfe, John R., and Goddeeris, John H. 1991. "Adverse Selection, Moral Hazard, and Wealth Effects in the Medigap Insurance Market." *Journal of Health Economics* 10:433–459.

INDEX

Aaron, Henry J., on British age-rationing, 105

Adverse selection: in aged population, 6; and annuities, 78, 81; as a consumption externality, 74; and CCRCs, 79, 122–123; and cross-subsidy in equilibrium, 72; defined, 68; and early purchase, 77, 79; evidence of, 80–83; and government insurance, 76, 77–78, 79–80; implications of model of, 75–79; and Life Care at Home, 124; and Long-Life Insurance, 124; with many risk classes, 74; and market failure, 74, 75, 76; and medigap insurance, 80; and monopoly, 74–75; and multiple-option plans, 82; and Pareto criterion, 73, 76; and RAMs, 79, 132; in Rand Experiment, 80; and scale economies, 79–80; and separating equilibrium, 72; theoretical model of, 70–75; and transition costs, 82; and vouchers, 103

Aged: economic status of, 10–12; needs for care of, 15–16; predominance of widows among, 16

Age pyramid: and birthrate, 14; and mortality, 14–15, 16; and oldest old, 16; shape of top of, 21; and specific birth cohorts, 14; squaring of, 12–17

Age-rationing: avoidance by saving, 107–108; of health care, 105–108; and health of young, 107; and intergenerational transfers, 135; and ordinary consumption, 107–108; as prudent choice, 106

Aging: as cause of death, 19; and disability, 36; and hospitalization, 3, 36–37; and nursing home residency, 3, 36–37; and physical change, 21; and physician visits, 36–37; of U.S. population, 12

Aid to Families of Dependent Children (AFDC), disruption of families by, 115

Annuities, 78, 81

Baby Boom generation: effects of size of, 2; reaching age 85, 36; low saving rate of, 5

Battin, Margaret P., on killing of and suicide by aged, 106

Bioactuarial models, 30–31

Birthrate: effect on age pyramid, 14; fluctuations in, 2; projections of, 14

Bishop, Christine, on long-term-care insurance prototype, 112

Board-and-care facilities, 123

Boskin, Michael J., Social Security Projections by, 43–44

Brody, Jacob A., on age-dependent risks, 17